The Natural Athlete

Eating to Win: The Athlete's Guide to Nutrition

ALAN LEWIS

CENTURY PUBLISHING/NEWMAN TURNER
LONDON

First published in Great Britain in 1984
by Century Publishing Co. Ltd,
Portland House,
12–13 Greek Street, London W1V 5LE

ISBN 0 7126 0942 3

Filmset by Deltatype, Ellesmere Port
Printed in Great Britain in 1984 by
Richard Clay Ltd, The Chaucer Press, Bungay, Suffolk

Alan Lewis is editor of *Here's Health*, Britain's leading natural living magazine. His career has included a spell as a full-time sports writer covering athletics, boxing and football. In 1972 he won the Provincial Journalist of the Year award for his coverage of the Olympic Games in Munich. He was chief news editor of the *Northamptonshire Evening Telegraph* and assistant editor of the Bedford County Press group of newspapers. For the past four years he has worked in the specialist area of health magazines and is editor-in-chief of Newman Turner Publications.

Also available from Century

The Bristol Diet Dr Alec Forbes
Death in the Locker Room Bob Goldman
Dieting Makes You Fat Geoffrey Cannon & Hetty Einzig
Fit for Nothing Martin Honeysett
The Food Scandal Caroline Walker & Geoffrey Cannon
Sprouting Beans and Seeds Judy Ridgway

Contents

Contents

Introduction

If you are involved in any kind of sport you are making special demands on your body.

You are expecting it to perform so that you can win.

And this could be at the weekly game of squash, football, cricket or tennis. Or it could be at the highest possible level of international sport – the Olympic Games.

What you are seeking is something extra – a few inches of speed, an ounce of strength, a few seconds' more stamina. You need this to make the difference between winning and losing, success and failure.

This book aims to provide the means to that extra performance, that something special sportsmen and sportswomen are straining for. It also seeks to do this in the best way: by preparing the body through a combination of correct diet backed up by the provision of extra vitamins and minerals – and also by advocating the right mental approach.

This is a combination which during the past three years has revolutionised many sports.

In 1984 every athlete appearing for Britain in the Olympic Games in Los Angeles went through a training programme which put as much emphasis on nutrition and diet as on physical preparation. And this was achieved in the face of accepting that it involved going back to basics – looking at an athlete's diet, how he or she ate and what they ate.

Programmes were planned with the help of experienced nutritionists and dieticians and the whole concept was as simple as possible – that to give peak performances athletes needed to be at the peak of their health and that meant a considerable improvement in their diet.

This programme heralded the era of the natural athlete – the man or woman who prepared on a better foundation than ever

1

before. It was a question of eating to win; learning that world-class performances cannot be expected on third-rate 'junk-food' fuel; realising the importance of food high in fibre, low in fats, low in sugar and low in salt; and learning that extra vitamins and minerals are essential for the very special demands being made on the body.

For twenty years the drug cloud which has hung over many athletic events has meant that performances have been materially affected by pharmaceutical means. The return to natural methods means that the athlete is reverting to concentration on his or her own inherited and trained qualities in order to achieve success.

The diet approach to success in sport works. And this is not only for those such as the members of Britain's elite Olympic athletics squad who are now convinced of its merits – men like Seb Coe, David Moorcroft, Daley Thompson and others. It also works in increasing the ability of the weekend sportsmen and sportswomen – whether they play squash, tennis, soccer, cricket or run or swim – to perform better.

The book is not only about the need to eat healthily but also about being able to reach a higher level of health and fitness, to recover from illness and injury quicker.

It's about running your body as a super-efficient machine.

How do you rate your diet?

If you had to give your diet a score out of ten, how would it rate?

Think about this for a moment or two and then run through the kind of food which features regularly in the diet of yourself and your family.

Now give your diet a mark out of ten.

If your score is above eight, then you are very exceptional – you not only know about all the things you need in order to eat well and stay healthy, but more important, you put this into regular practice.

However, most of us have to face up to the fact that we are well below that score.

In fact, a recent major report on Britain's diet gave a score of no more than four out of ten. In a significant and controversial report published in 1983, the National Advisory Committee on Nutrition Education (NACNE) laid down proposals for nutritional guidelines for health in Britain.

What this report said was that as a nation we needed to cut down drastically on the amounts of sugar, fat and salt that we ate, and at the same time significantly to increase the amount of fibre in our diet.

It was a document which was nothing more than damning about the food we eat, with overtones of 'do better – or else' running through its pages.

A good diet is something everyone should be aiming for – whether or not they are involved in sport or regular exercise. The problem is that there is no easy or magic formula. It's not possible to put all the information into a computer and come out with all the right answers.

Each of us varies in terms of what we need, what we like, the risks we run in harming our health and the sheer practical problems of trying to organise an adequate diet.

Yet most of us do have a vague idea about the link between the way we eat and the way we feel, even if this goes no further than a worrying feeling that gorging a large wedge of chocolate cake covered with lashings of cream cannot really be doing us a great deal of good.

The problem is that chocolate cake happens to taste nice. We know what we like, but knowing what we need is not all that easy.

So any starting point has to be – how good or how bad is your own diet?

Is it good enough to enable your body to perform as it should?

If you are not aware of the immense influence that food can have on the way your body functions, then all you have to do is consider the link between our over-refined, processed diet and the major illnesses of the Western world.

Not all our modern ills can be blamed on food. The irony is that in Western countries the balance has swung too far. Nowadays we rarely encounter diseases caused by nutritional deficiencies or people starving to death. The quality of our food has made us strong enough to fight off many of the infectious diseases which were killers less than a hundred years ago.

Ironically, therefore, our diet is too good for our own health. It damages our bodies and our way of life. Our lives are not as healthy as they could be and we fail to get as much as we should from the wonderful machines that we know as our bodies.

Coronary heart disease is the commonest cause of death in Western countries, killing one man in four. Factors such as smoking, lack of exercise, high blood pressure and a history of such illness in the family have an important bearing so far as heart disease is concerned, but experts are now convinced that diet is the crucial factor in its prevention.

Before the First World War this was a rare disease in the West; all the evidence available indicates that between 1880 and 1904 the death rate from coronary heart disease was approximately 22 per million of the population. By 1915 the level had reached 35 per million and by 1930, 148 per million.

Figures for the present day are over 3100 per million. True, a significant improvement in the ability to diagnose heart disease came to the forefront in the 1930s. Consequently some people whose deaths had previously been attributed to 'a cause unknown' could now be seen to have suffered from heart problems. Even so, the rise is staggering and it is an epidemic which has continued unabated to the present day. Yet coronary heart disease is still almost unknown among rural Africans and is rare in most communities in Asia.

It's a fairly sobering thought that if you are over forty you have a fifty-fifty chance of having a heart attack – and that if you get a heart attack you have a 30-percent chance of dying within the first twenty-four hours.

The link between the diet and the disease is clearly defined and medically established.

Moreover, if heart-related problems can be such killers, it is only a short step to work out the damage being done to millions more people which while not fatal still causes pain and distress and leaves the body performing badly. Arteries supply blood to the heart. The problem with these small arteries is that if they get blocked up the results are immediately felt and the damage is often serious. They become 'furred up' as a result of a fatty substance that includes cholesterol. Although some cholesterol comes from foods which contain it such as butter and eggs, the body makes most of its cholesterol out of fats in the food one eats, especially saturated fats.

What you need to do with your diet is to cut back on fatty foods. The most dramatic and effective way to achieve this is by reducing the amount of animal fats you eat – butter cream, fatty meat, lard and so on. Remember there are also 'hidden fats' in processed meats like sausages and meat pies, fried foods, chocolate and cheese.

However, the odds are that when you consider your own diet it is still too high in fats. Give some thought to the number of animal fats you have every day.

Do you eat bacon for breakfast? How often do you have butter, cream, even top-of-the-milk? How much fried food do you eat? How much pork or lamb (both exceptionally high in fats)?

This is one of the most important questions when you start investigating how your own diet rates.

Defining the role of diet as a contributory factor in causing cancer is not as easy, although evidence is mounting that too much fat can increase the risk of developing certain cancers. And it is important to remember that cancer is not one disease but many; it has about two hundred identifiable forms with which different factors of the diet are linked in various ways. The most common form in North America and Britain, with the exception

5

of lung cancer, attributed to cigarette smoking, is cancer of the large bowel; there is no other type so closely related to economic development and our way of life. Interestingly, in Africa and Asia it is much less common than in the West.

Cancer of the large bowel is a disease which seems to sum up in a tragic way the typical high-fat, low-fibre diet which too many people still have. One explanation more widely accepted now is that the cancer could come from some bacteria in the waste matter passing through the colon, which produces a substance causing the disease.

A low-fibre diet causes food to pass through the body system very slowly; possibly that process produces more concentrated carcinogens, which remain in contact with the lining of the rectum and colon for a long time.

It seems unlikely that this form of cancer is caused by carcinogenic foods or chemicals, because in that case we should also be prone to cancer in the small bowel and this does not happen.

Cutting down on the fats in your diet and stepping up the fibre intake will reduce the threat of this form of cancer – that involves taking more wholewheat cereals, bread, pasta and crispbread, also more nuts, dried fruits, fresh fruit and vegetables.

But it is not only heart disease and cancer which have a link with diet. Our present diet also encourages illnesses such as gallstones, diabetes and strokes.

The presence of gallstones is one of the commonest diseases in developed countries. They used to be seen only in rich people – now they occur in all classes. Likewise they used to be a disease of middle age – now they are found at all ages and in Sweden operations for the removal of gallstones in children are not uncommon. As populations change from eating high-fibre diets to refined diets, the incidence of gallstones increases dramatically.

Women are still the main victims, although whereas once a typical patient used to be 'fat, fertile and forty', in 1984 she is more likely to be young, taking oral contraceptives and dieting. Gallstones are hard deposits of calcium salts and cholesterol which form within the gall-bladder. A high percentage of them cause no trouble at all, but the problem arises when they move out of the gall-bladder and into the bile duct. This happens to about one-third of all gallstones and when it does the process can be a very painful one which necessitates an operation.

In fact, the operation for the removal of the gall-bladder is the most common non-urgent operation in the Western world – about one million are removed every year. More money is spent on removing gallstones in the United States than on all medical services on the continent of Africa.

In the West the disease has a number of classic situations. For example, girls who are dieting often cut out carbohydrate foods like bread and potatoes. They may also go on a fast, cutting out food altogether. Fasting tends to raise the cholesterol saturation of the bile and cutting out starchy foods means cutting fibre intake; this leads to lower production of bile salts and greater risk of gallstones.

The diet approach needed to avoid gallstones includes plenty of wholegrain cereals and foods high in fibre. If you are overweight, then choose a sensible nutritious diet and don't get involved in fasting.

There is considerable evidence to suggest that the link between diet and diabetes – another of the major diseases of the twentieth century – is a vital one. Low-fat, high-fibre diets have given the control of diabetes a new direction.

In Britain today, one-in-twenty people below the age of fifty and three-in-twenty over fifty may be considered diabetic. The illness is really about inability to control the amount of glucose in the blood by normal metabolic means.

Those who develop diabetes under the age of forty are not able to make enough insulin and have to be treated by drugs. Of those who develop it in later life, it is more common in people who are overweight. It can often be treated by taking tablets.

Diabetes became increasingly common during the nineteenth century and the early part of the twentieth century. In Britain, diabetes mortality rates fell during the food shortage of the First World War. It has been suggested that the drop in the intake of sugar-rich, processed foods and a return to more home-made unrefined food was the principal cause. Again, it can be seen to be a 'new' disease which has flourished because of our present way of life. Widespread studies from all over the world show diabetes to be very rare in rural populations eating unrefined foods.

Before the discovery of insulin, the only way of treating diabetes was by severely restricting the intake of carbohydrates, starch and sugar, which meant that only a little glucose was released into the bloodstream. While this may have been effective once, the fact is that too much carbohydrate in the diet is not the cause of diabetes.

The key to dietary control is to be found in dietary fibre, and the reason for its having such a dramatic effect is tied up with the question of blood sugar control. When sugars are taken in by diabetics, it is difficult for them to cope with the resulting sudden increase in blood sugar. Fibre in foods slows down the absorption of sugar and so a diet which has plenty of fibre in it provides the best chance of achieving really good control of the disease. The other half of the diet equation is to cut back on the amount of fat. By lowering the quantity of fat in the diet the diabetic is replacing high-calorie foods with more protein and carbohydrate; this means that it is easier to reach and maintain ideal body weight, an important goal for the diabetic.

Apart from the major killers and illnesses, there are other diet-related ailments such as migraine, allergies, low resistance and a general feeling of being below par.

If the food we eat can be traced back to demonstrate its dramatic effect on the growth of such illnesses as heart diseases, cancer, diabetes and so on, then it should not be difficult to appreciate how powerful a tool is diet in the way we live and perform. Eating the right foods in the right amounts is perhaps the simplest and most effective way to stay healthy. More important to the person such as an athlete, who is demanding so much of his or her body in terms of performance, is the way it can be used.

Dr David Healey is one of the new generation of nutritionists who has worked in hospitals in London, New York and Sweden on the effects of diet on disease. He also led a study group to Africa to investigate the effect of an increasingly 'Western diet' being made available to people who lived on traditionally unrefined foods. He comments:

For the past fifty years the role of dietary medicine has been one of curing deficiency diseases. For a long time it ignored the overwhelming fact that the foods we ate weren't just not helping us but were killing us.

The past ten years have seen us now accepting the truth that most of our commonest diseases are food related and a very, very large part of the effect they have can be avoided by us getting to know more about the food we eat and the effect it has on it.

The explosion of that information has been huge. The message is getting through. It's not as fast as it could be and there is still a lot of work to be done in improving the quality of the diet. The Government has accepted it. The NACNE report will have an effect. It has laid down what we must do. I think that some of the recommendations on the amount of sugar we should cut back, the amount of fat we should cut back and the need for us to step up the fibre in our diet and take less salt have all been underestimated. It's not that we don't need to do it, we need to do it quicker.

The most harmful changes that have happened to our diet have been the replacement of carbohydrate foods, such as wholemeal bread and cereals, with fat and animal fat in particular and highly processed foods which contain harmful and damaging additives, preservatives and colourings. The development of "junk food" has been significant.

But we have to look on the positive side and tell people that the evidence is there and it is simple to act on. Take the example of comparing lung cancer with atherosclerosis, two major killers.

Lung cancer has been shown beyond question to be the result of cigarette smoking. Giving up smoking will drastically reduce lung cancer but not totally eliminate it as there are other causes. Ninety-five per cent of lung cancer patients are smokers and 70 per cent smoke more than twenty cigarettes a day. The chances of getting lung cancer increase dramatically as the rate of smoking goes up. Clearly to smoke damages your health.

Atherosclerosis is just as much caused by eating badly as lung cancer is by smoking. If you eat junk food high in fats, high in cholesterol, the flow of blood to the heart muscle will deteriorate. The result is angina or a heart attack. The evidence is there.

Dr Healey, himself a marathon runner, has spent much of his time in the past two years working with athletic groups and clubs on providing diet help and information:

I want to take the diet approach a stage further into an equally positive side. We need to educate people about how diet can control major illnesses, but we also need to educate people that diet can help those people who are not ill.

9

What I have been looking at is the effect of improving the diet of people who are already fit. I've been to athletics clubs and talked to club athletes as well as international athletes. They are all extremely fit people. Their diet in many cases is appalling. They do live on junk food. Hours and hours are spent training to develop muscles and to develop speed. Yet after a training programme it's back to a bar of chocolate or fish and chips.

It is all out of proportion and it doesn't reflect the importance of what athletes are eating. I believe 90 per cent of the athletes in this country have been operating below par not because of their training schedules, but because of the food they eat.

It's a subjective view to pass on to them. I appreciate athletes don't have a lot of time. But it can be organised, they can combine eating a balanced, nutritious diet within their training schedule.

It can help the club athlete, the weekend squash player or the committed international athlete. It's all to do with getting the message over. I think there is a great need to develop the importance of diet to the fit person just as much as to the ill person. It has been neglected too much.

Dr Healey and other nutritionists have stressed that everyone ought to look at his or her diet. As far as the athlete is concerned, the odds are heavily against your diet being good enough for the demands being made on your body.

Having no time is no excuse!

Eating to win

The best athletes in the world now concede that correct diet is 90 per cent of the battle.

They know this because they have seen it work. In the build-up to the 1984 Los Angeles Olympic Games more world class athletes than ever before – faced with the pressure of expected success and the fear of stricter drug control – have turned to the natural approach to achieve that extra edge.

They have begun to eat to win.

Brian Hooper, one of the world's fittest athletes, shot to international recognition and fame through winning television's 'Superstars' competition – first the British and International contests and then the World finals. 'Superstars' is a unique blend of up to ten different sports chosen from swimming, cycling, sprinting, weight-lifting, basketball, gymnasium tests and an obstacle race.

As a pole vaulter, Brian was one of the longest serving members of the British international squad. His success was built on strong foundations: four hours training, six days a week, backed up by a health food regime and a scientifically designed programme of vitamins and minerals.

He is a committed 'whole-fooder', an athlete who avoids sugar. His diet is high in unrefined carbohydrates such as wholemeal bread and he eats plenty of vegetables and fruit. In his opinion:

Correct nutrition is 90 per cent of the battle. At that level if you're even one per cent off physically you could be up to 50 per cent off mentally and that could cost you an event.

It comes down to you being properly rested: you have to make sure you are looking after your diet as well as possible, so that your body gets all the nutrients it needs to recover.

11

At twenty-eight years of age and at a stage when most athletes are winding down their careers, he discovered wholefoods and subsequently set five British pole vault records. He was invited to take part in the 'Superstars' competition during what was to be quite a year for athletics. He had to train hard for the competition – which incidentally wins a regular worldwide audience of millions – but since he began to participate, Brian Hooper has been unbeatable.

At one time this outstanding athlete was ready to give up athletics, but after re-vamping his diet he noticed such an improvement that he decided to persevere. For him the benefits of wholefoods and supplements bring a number of advantages, such as fewer injuries and illnesses; quicker recovery after training sessions and the capacity to maintain peak performances for longer.

His views about the importance of nutrition are no longer unique among athletes.

Before the start of the crucial 1984 athletics season, a special nutrition seminar for athletic coaches was held at Crystal Palace; the emphasis was on the importance of athletes' diets in order that they should be able to prepare their bodies correctly.

The message here was that 1984 was the year during which the athletes should reach new physical heights and optimal health by means of a closer analysis and understanding of what they eat.

'The temptation is for athletes to eat convenience foods and keep stocked up with sugary snacks and drinks,' said one nutritionist to the British Olympic team. 'Just processing that sort of intake robs the body of essential nutrients such as the B-complex vitamins which sportsmen need in great amounts because of energy production, muscle repair, oxygen transport and stress controls.'

So how good is the average athlete's diet?

Oxford nutritionist Pamela Clark worked with members of the British international team preparing for the Los Angeles Olympic Games and has compared the diets with club athletes. She paints a black picture.

Far too many athletes think that to get extra energy they have to eat plenty of sugar, sugary food and stack up with protein. There's far too little emphasis being put on unrefined carbohydrates, vegetables and fruit.

I have to say that the athletes I have been working with have

12

tried to reach high levels of performance in competition when their bodies are operating inefficiently because of their diet. They are not getting the maximum endurance and performance levels.

What is needed is something of a diet revolution. Athletes don't have much time. They do abuse their diet by filling in odd moments with poor quality food. To eat properly doesn't take a lot of time or effort. What it does take is the knowledge of the sort of foods to eat in what amounts.

She emphasised that there was little doubt that diet could help to provide athletes with an extra edge to their performances:

We've seen it in our research. People who before had made no effort with what they ate and were on basically junk food had problems with recovery after training. They had a large number of interruptions in their training programmes with colds and infections.

They were asking a lot of their bodies and the preparation was poor. We've now converted those athletes to wholefoods, taught them the basics of cutting down on fat, increasing fibre and leaving sugar from their diets.

I would think that eight out of ten are much happier with the way they feel and the way they perform.

The diet approach is one which can have the maximum effect on international standard athletes, but the principle remains true for the club athlete or indeed anyone who is involved in sport or even jogging for pleasure.

If you have already examined your diet, then now is the time for action.

There are four starting points which need your attention:

1 Reduce the amount of fat in your diet
2 Increase the fibre
3 Cut out sugar
4 Cut back on the salt you take
5 Eat less processed foods

Each one will have a dramatic effect on the condition of your body. Each has a vital role to play in exploiting the potential of your body to achieve improved performance.

Facts about fat

It is very easy to eat too much fat – and most of us do so.

The aim should be to cut down your fat intake to 80g a day – and that is actually more than you need. The problem is that it is so easy to eat too many fats; they are hidden in high amounts in foods such as biscuits, cakes, chocolate, crisps, ice cream, meat, nuts, pastries and processed meat products such as meat pies and sausages.

Fats are a very concentrated source of energy. It is because a little contains so much energy that too much is laid down as body waste rather than being burnt up.

The fats that accumulate on the inner walls of blood vessels are a critical factor in heart disease, which is such a killer in the Western world. The villain is cholesterol in the bloodstream. So what can you do about it? First, you need to understand how the fat we eat works in the body.

There are three families of fatty acids – saturated, monosaturated and polyunsaturated. Each fatty acid molecule consists of atoms of carbon, hydrogen and oxygen arranged in a specific pattern.

When there is hydrogen at every available spot in the molecule, the fatty acid is *saturated*.

When some hydrogen is missing, the molecule is not saturated but *unsaturated*.

If just one molecule of hydrogen is missing, the fatty acid is *monosaturated*. Olive oil, for example, is a monosaturated fat.

If, however, two or more molecules of hydrogen are missing the molecule is *polyunsaturated*. Corn oil is a polyunsaturated fat.

Results of major studies into the different effects of fatty acids go to show that saturated fats are the 'bad guys' in encouraging high levels of cholesterol in the blood. Polyunsaturated fats may help to reduce blood cholesterol, while monosaturated fats seem to be neutral in this respect.

Saturated fatty acids are mostly found in animal products and unsaturated fatty acids in plant products. That is a broad general rule, although there are of course exceptions.

Healthful polyunsaturated fats to include in your diet are:

14

- safflower oil – 74 per cent polyunsaturated
- sunflower oil – 64 per cent
- corn oil – 58 per cent
- soybean oil – 57 per cent

You can see that the oils high in polyunsaturates tend to be liquid at room temperature. Compare the list above with such saturated fats as:

- lard
- butter
- many margarines

Some plant fats do happen to be high in the wrong kind of fats, but these are items such as coconut oil and palm oil which are very much the exception to the rule.

There is little doubt that being fat exposes you to unnecessary illnesses such as heart disease, high blood pressure, diabetes and cancer. What is more relevant, though less dramatically obvious, is that it reduces the ability of the heart to perform well.

For athletes, eating too much fat means wasted energy; it isn't effective. Few athletes at the top level need to worry about being overweight, but they should worry about utilising their food to the maximum. To have too many fats in the diet does not constitute a very effective training and energy building tool.

For the average weekend player – whether the sport is soccer, squash or tennis – weight could well be a problem. The fatter you get, the less effective your body becomes and the less efficiently your immune system protects you against infection and early ageing.

All the evidence points strongly to there being a firm link between heart disease and a high level of cholesterol in the blood; this in turn is linked to a diet rich in fats, especially saturated fats.

In countries where the average saturated fat intake is just over 30g per day, as in parts of Asia and Africa, heart disease is rare. Many developed countries have a fat intake of 110g a day however, and heart disease is common and deadly.

Athletes often base a large part of their eating plan on plenty of red meat and eggs, and are confused by conflicting reports regarding diet, blood cholesterol and heart disease and the effective working of the heart. The cholesterol controversy – whether the cholesterol you eat influences the level of cholesterol in your blood – remains unresolved. Nevertheless, it is worth pointing out the following:

- Eating a high cholesterol diet has been shown to be the usual cause of high blood cholesterol
- Even with a low cholesterol diet your body can produce excessive amounts of cholesterol as long as your diet is high in saturated fats such as butter, beef, pork, cakes and chocolate
- When your diet is low in the saturated animal fats but high in polyunsaturated fats, the blood cholesterol drops

There has been a great deal of argument about the advisability of a switch to a diet high in polyunsaturated fats. Organisations which have been seen to have an interest in the outcome of the controversy from a purely commercial point of view have claimed that a diet high in polyunsaturates could be bad for you.

The evidence is that although there may be a long-term effect as a result of eating too many polyunsaturated fats, none has been found which is as serious as heart disease.

Therefore what is suggested is that it is desirable to exchange some saturated fats for polyunsaturated fats.

Athletes' twenty-point plan to cut down on fat

- Read the labels on processed foods and cut back on those where fat comes near the top of the list of ingredients
- Never fry food if you can avoid it
- Eat potatoes baked, boiled or mashed with no extra milk or butter, rather than chips
- Switch to recipes which have less meat, dishes built around beans and pulses
- Eat less of the very fatty meats like lamb and pork; choose fish and chicken instead
- Use salad or low-fat fillings such as cottage cheese, instead of meat or cheese in sandwiches and rolls
- Stop adding butter and margarine to vegetables
- Instead of drinking whole milk, try fresh skimmed milk or switch to fruit or vegetable juice instead
- Cut off all visible fat from meat before cooking. Cut off the skin from chicken joints before casseroling

- Use skimmed instead of whole milk in tea and coffee
- Use polyunsaturated margarine instead of butter on bread
- Switch to a low-fat cheese. Avoid cream cheese (47 per cent fat), Stilton (40 per cent), Cheddar (38 per cent), but try cottage cheese (4 per cent)
- Cut out chocolate from your diet – replace it with fresh fruit and vegetables
- Cut out cakes and pastries and try a low-fat yoghurt or fruit as an alternative
- Use polyunsaturated fats instead of lard, butter or other margarines in cooking. Safflower oil is an excellent alternative
- Grill rather than fry meat. Don't use the meat dripping for gravy
- If a recipe calls for cream, try natural yoghurt instead
- Moisten sandwiches with salad instead of butter or margarine
- Use a non-stick pan so that you can get away with using less fat when you do have to fry. Also, remember to use polyunsaturated fats
- Cut down the fat in pastry making – one part fat to three parts flour rather than two to one.

There is a double danger involved with junk food, which many athletes have to turn to because of the pressures of time and the priority given to training as opposed to diet.

Junk food means a diet which is high in fat – most popular of the junk foods are hamburgers, chips, cakes and pastries – and low in vitamins, minerals and essential nutrients. In a bid to get more of the latter, nutrition demands more calories. Overeating then produces more poisonous wastes than the body can dispose of and so it stows them away in the layer of fat under the skin.

For the athlete the problem is straightforward. Fat cells are far less active than any other cells in the body. They burn less energy; they are less efficient and they contribute less to the way in which the body performs. This means that the more fat you have relative to muscle, the lower your metabolic rate.

The typical British diet is too high in unsaturated fats and cholesterol, hence the average person in this country is prone not only to heart disease but to the poor functioning of their hearts.

Athletes are not immune to this. A recent assessment of diet at one of our major training colleges highlighted the fact that too much fat was a standard part of the day-to-day diets of young athletes and that they were carrying too much dead weight.

Of even more concern, however, is the danger to weekend sportsmen and women, especially men who insist on participating in strenuous sporting activity despite being overweight.

Sports such as squash, soccer and sprinting over-stretch the heart over short periods. Early in 1984, the dangers of playing squash for men whose heart rate could not cope with it were highlighted in a medical report, which stressed that people were dying of heart attacks on the squash courts. They were overweight and unprepared for such dramatic demands on their bodies, which were pushing their hearts to breaking point.

Eating too much fat is not only dangerous but it is contributing nothing to your bid to achieve improved standards and better results from your body.

Facts about fibre

If you are eating to win, then you need to know about fibre. More important, you will need to increase the quantity of fibre in your diet.

The story of fibre is so simple that it is hardly believable. The fact that many of our modern diseases are caused by eating too many of the nutrients in foods and not enough of the roughage, is very basic. Yet it has fired the imagination of scientists and doctors all over the world.

More than a thousand scientific papers have now been published on the subject, and with the vast amount of publicity fibre has been given over the past ten years it is hardly surprising that it has caught on with the public.

If you are eating for your health, then fibre does assume a critical importance.

Fibre is frequently removed from cereals and until recently was regarded as worthless by doctors and nutritionists.

The change-round in opinion has been dramatic. It is now claimed that fibre in the diet can help to protect against a list of illnesses and diseases – from heart disease to some forms of cancer to appendicitis, to diabetes. According to different theories, this is achieved by reducing the time that waste stays in our systems and diluting the toxins produced as food passes through the body.

The report of the National Advisory Committee on Nutrition Education into Britain's nutritional and health guidelines has indicated that we should all eat more fibre.

Another report from the Royal College of Physicians strengthens that view. The term 'dietary fibre' was in fact only formally adopted in the early 1970s, so there is some excuse for thinking that all the fuss is about something new.

The concept of roughage in our food and the dangers if it is removed date back to Hippocrates, who found that white flour causes illnesses in the bowel.

For centuries the fibre story has centred on bread, because for so long this has been the staple food in Britain. Most of the poor ate little but bread and the story of fibre begins with the demand of the rich for whiter bread which they thought would be free from impurities.

Its history since that time has been surrounded by controversy. Scientists in the thirties and forties were concerned not with the bran content of the foods we ate but with the nutritional content. Thousands of doctors advised their patients to switch to a low-fibre diet.

Two men in particular have played an important part in the story so far. One is Dr T. R. (Tom) Allinson, who qualified in medicine at the age of twenty-three and started experimenting with the effects of diet on disease. He felt so strongly about food that he spent a great deal of time writing about it for the public. This and the open and violent way in which he attacked the danger of drugs made him something of an outcast from the medical profession. Struck off the register by the British Medical Association, after an expensive legal battle he decided to change direction and bought up a mill in London's East End. He could now control not only the quality but – more important to him – the content of his own bread. He was also able to provide good wholemeal flour in a pre-packaged form so that people could make their own bread.

The effect of Allinson's activities was dramatic. Knowledge of his beliefs spread and others became convinced of the importance of fibre. Today his name is known by millions. The Allinson mill in Castleford, Yorkshire is now the largest stone-ground mill in the world. It is owned by Britain's biggest health food company, Booker Health Foods, and flour from the mill goes to make

Allinson wholemeal bread, one of the top-selling brands in Britain.

The second character who played a major part in the fibre story is Surgeon-Captain T. L. Cleave.

As the senior medical officer on board the battleship *King George V* during the Second World War, Cleave found that the majority of the men were constipated and were suffering accordingly. Other remedies were either not available or too expensive, so he gave them miller's bran. Since it could not be classed as a drug, the men were forced to pay for it themselves – and they did so happily. Captain Cleave built up a philosophy of medicine during the next fourteen years and in 1956 published what is now held to be the original paper on the dangers of refined carbohydrates and disease. He was terrified of the dangers in sugar and white flour when all the goodness and purity had been taken out. He pointed to the horror behind eating a purified manufactured chemical such as sugar; to the changes it caused in digestion; to the possibility that it could produce vitamin deficiency diabetes and even cause cancer.

Other men have been significant in the unfolding of the story. In 1964 London surgeon Neil Painter took the bold step of defying the orthodox medical books by announcing that low fibre foods were bad for the bowel. Dr Dennis Burkitt brought zeal and enthusiasm to the subject of fibre and related it in particular to the healthier diets of countries like Africa and Asia where refined foods were rare. By comparison, the fibre-depleted and fat-rich diet of the West was seen by him as the cause of many illnesses.

Therefore there is an element of the pioneering spirit behind the discovery of the benefits of fibre to our diet.

What has happened is that as people become more affluent, they tend to eat more meat and animal products and fewer of the stable starchy foods such as bread and potatoes.

Dietary fibre is a broad term for a large number of substances that make up the supporting structure in plant cell walls. These mostly pass unchanged and unhindered through the digestive system.

The best-known source of fibre is cereal grains. The outer covering or husk of the grain accounts for about 13 per cent of its total. One of the special properties of cells in this husk is their ability to take up and retain water, which could explain some of the beneficial effects of dietary fibre. In refined or white flour the husk is removed as part of the milling process, the discarded material being known as bran.

The actual fibre content of bran can be as high as 50 per cent, which makes it the richest source of fibre available — but not necessarily the best or most palatable way of increasing fibre.

Bran contains only one group of fibres; fruit and vegetables contain vitamins and minerals too and other wholefoods contain starch as well. Therefore the best plan is to eat more fibre-rich foods rather than those to which bran has been added.

The growth in the popularity of wholemeal flour reflects the public's interest in bran. Wholemeal flour and bread ought to be a key part of your diet. Forget about white bread and white flour —it does you no good!

Brown rice, wholemeal pasta, pastry and breakfast cereals made from whole grains are a good source of fibre. Fruit and vegetables contain less fibre than cereals, but because we eat a lot of them they make a vital contribution to the amount of fibre we eat.

Today high-fibre diets are very much in fashion and a book on the merits of fibre — The F-Plan Diet by Audrey Eyton — became a national best seller. The need for fibre is crucial to any eating plan designed to improve your health. If you took action on other aspects of your diet but ignored fibre, the plan would not work.

When marathon runners come to tackle the question of carbohydrate loading, then fibre becomes even more important. For it is unrefined carbohydrates (complex) which are needed, high in fibre content, which mean that starch and not sugar is digested and used by the body.

Dr Dennis Burkitt puts the importance of fibre into context:

It can be compared to stationing an ambulance at the foot of a cliff to pick up casualties as men and women fall over and sustain injuries of various kinds. The efficient ambulance takes the patients to medical centres equipped with all modern facilities and staffed with highly trained medical teams. But how much better it would be to erect a fence round the top of the cliff to prevent people falling off in the first place.

The effects of fibre in our food are nothing short of dramatic. An international convention reviewing recent research on fibre in Oslo concluded:

What we have to look at in the future is the importance of fibre not only in preventing disease but improving the quality of life amongst people who are not ill. A diet rich in fibre has been seen to rebuild the ability of man to cope with disease. What we now need is evidence that the sophisticated machinery of a man and woman's body can be fine-tuned by such a diet. There is everything to suggest such is the case.

Around 30g a day would seem to be a reasonable target for the amount of fibre in your diet. At the moment, people in industrialised countries are eating on average 20g a day, as compared with over 60g a day for the typical rural African or Asian.

For the weekend sportsman and sportswoman, the added importance of fibre is in its capacity to make slimming that much easier. A wholefood diet which is high in fibre content and low in fat will make it much easier to get down to 'fighting weight' and to maintain it.

A whole range of fibre products in supplement form is now on the market, which provide bran in tablet form. They remain natural products based mainly on plants high in fibre content, aimed at the next generation of fibre lovers.

These are significant for people who suffer from allergies to the gluten in wheat, barley, rye and oats and who need to obtain fibre from other sources.

Such products are mainly sold for the benefit of slimmers or as a convenient way of taking fibre when on holiday, especially abroad.

The following plan sets out some rough guidelines to adopt in order to improve your diet by increasing the fibre content.

Athletes' seven-point plan for eating more fibre and starch

- Eat brown rice and wholemeal pasta and leave skin on potatoes
- Eat more pulses (lentils, beans and peas). Use them more often in a wide range of recipes including soups and stews
- Switch to wholemeal bread and crispbreads
- Eat more fruit and vegetables
- Eat a proper high-fibre breakfast using muesli. Make your

own from oats, fresh and dried fruits, nuts and wheatgerm
- Add bran to soups, crumbles and pastry mixes
- If you are eating snacks, switch to high-fibre fruit or bran bars

When you are eating bran or stepping up the fibre in your diet, it is often wise to drink more water. Dry forms of fibre such as bran, wholemeal flour and bread absorb a considerable amount of water and this has to be replaced.

The list which follows provides useful information with respect to the actual percentage of fibre contained in a wide range of foods.

The fibre in your food

CEREALS	%
Wheat bran (miller's bran)	44.0
Wholemeal flour (100% unrefined)	9.6
Brown flour (85% refined)	7.5
White flour (72% refined)	3.0
Soya flour (low fat)	14.3
Sweetcorn, canned	5.7
Corn-on-the-cob, boiled	4.7
Rice, white, polished, boiled	0.8
Rice, brown, unpolished, boiled	5.5

BREAD	
Wholemeal	8.5
Brown	5.1
Hovis (UK)	4.6
White	2.7

BREAKFAST CEREALS	
All Bran	26.7
Puffed Wheat	15.4
Weetabix	12.7
Shredded Wheat	12.3
Cornflakes	11.0
Muesli	7.4
Grapenuts	7.0
Sugar Puffs	6.1
Special K	5.5
Rice Krispies	4.5
Porridge	0.8

BISCUITS	
Crispbread rye (Ryvita)	11.7
Digestive, plain	5.5
Wheat starch-reduced crispbread (Energen)	4.9
Shortbread	2.1

NUTS	
Almonds	14.3
Coconut, fresh	13.6
Brazil	9.0
Peanuts	8.1
Hazel	6.1

LEAF VEGETABLES	%
Spinach, boiled	6.3
Broccoli tops, boiled	2.9
Spring greens, boiled	3.8
Brussel sprouts, boiled	2.9
Cabbage, boiled	1.8
Cauliflower, boiled	1.8
Celery, raw	1.8
Lettuce	1.5

ROOT VEGETABLES	
Horseradish, raw	8.3
Carrots, boiled	3.0
Carrots, raw	2.9
Parsnips, boiled	2.5
Beetroots, boiled	2.5
Potatoes, baked in skins (flesh only)	2.5
Potatoes boiled (new)	2.0

LEGUMES	
Peas, frozen, boiled	12.0
Beans, haricot (whole-beans, boiled, (baked and canned)	7.4
Beans, in tomato sauce	7.3
Peas, canned	6.3
Peas, fresh, boiled	5.2
Broad beans, boiled	5.1
Lentils, split, boiled	3.7
Runner beans, boiled	3.4

FRUITS	
Dates, dried	8.7
Blackberries	7.3
Raisins	6.8
Cranberries	4.2
Bananas	3.4
Pears, fresh, eating	3.3
Strawberries	2.2
Plums, raw, eating	2.1
Apples	2.0
Oranges	2.0
Tomatoes, raw	1.5
Pineapple, fresh	1.2
Grapefruit	0.6

The drug approach – will it ever end?

The lists of world and Olympic athletics records make impressive reading.

People are continually running faster, throwing further, jumping higher.

The fact is, however, that the present record lists would have to be completely rewritten if drug offenders were to be removed.

The use of drugs by athletes in the pursuit of better performances has been critical. It has cut at the very heart of athletics competition and one can only guess the extent of the effect of drugs on performances and achievements.

Up to the 1960s there were differences in environment which affected how athletes performed: Kenyans living at high altitude had advantages. Communist countries giving state support put their athletes in a better position to train and perform and removed their financial worries. But apart from that, an athlete depended on his or her own inherited and trained qualities in order to achieve success.

There was no hint of the revolution which was to come, no hint that an athlete could have his performance levels materially affected by pharmaceutical means.

In 1984, however, it is no longer possible to accept any world class performance, outside the main endurance events, as having been achieved without the influence of drugs. In the build-up to the 1984 Olympic Games in Los Angeles, where the potential rewards for success in front of huge worldwide television audiences were enormous, the chances of detection were minimal and the punishments nominal for athletes without scruples in this respect.

The use of drugs in sport has become commonplace during the past twenty years. The best-known are the anabolic steroids, which help the body to absorb huge doses of muscle-building protein when linked to a strict training regime. They improve work rate and provide a stimulus.

The improvement in the major throwing events for both men and women has been dramatic since the introduction of anabolic steroids in the 1960s. Since the 1960 Rome Olympics, average body weights have gone up by 24kg (52lb) in men and 10kg (22lb) in women, although the average heights of the competitors has remained constant.

The record books reflect the change. In the thirty years up to 1962 the world record in the women's shot increased by 12 ft. During the past twenty years, however, it has been lengthened by another 20 ft. Similar increases have been recorded in every major throwing event. This reflects an unnatural development of the body in the athletes taking part and in the performances they can produce.

It would be wrong to concentrate on the 'heavy' events, which have been more noticeable because of the dramatic change in the appearances of the athletes in pure physique terms. Steroids have also affected every event in the speed — power area. Proven cases of drug abuse have been found in athletics, but other sports including swimming have been under suspicion as having an involvement in drugs.

The International Amateur Athletics Federation which has stepped up its programme of drug detection, has done so in the face of public outrage and the need to defend the sport. Several athletes have been suspended, but allowed to return to their sport after a twelve-month ban.

An internal memorandum was circulated last year amongst members of the International Olympic Medical Committee. This was confidential and in response to concern within the committee that not enough was being done to increase the ability to detect drugs at the 1984 Los Angeles Olympic Games.

The document gave the assurance that more sophisticated methods for analysing and detecting drugs would be available in Los Angeles. Drug control units, it noted, had been operating throughout America:

It will not be the case that we will merely test for drugs at the Games themselves. Our programme, using control and detection units, has been operating for over a year at major and secondary events. We feel this is the only sure deterrent.

What the medical committee has been saying is, 'We will test for drugs at random events during the calendar year. Our policy is not to frighten athletes because they fear detection. Our policy is to inform and educate in terms of the dangers of damage to the system in later life. We accept the temptation of drugs is too great for many competitors.'

In the past, drug detection has been criticised in that it only occurs at major competitions such as the Olympic Games, when offending athletes have been off steroids for a sufficiently long time for the drug to have been cleared from their bodies.

Steroids are essentially training drugs for which it has been virtually pointless to test at major competitions. The significant change since the 1980 Moscow Olympic Games is that in the United States the tests are now carried out at University training grounds and squad training weekends. The effect of these new tactics has been said by one senior administrator to have been 'shattering'.

In Britain, the Chelsea College drug control unit, part of the University of London, is at the forefront of combating drug abuse in sport. At the head of its research programme is Professor Arnold Beckett, a former president of the Pharmaceutical Society who has brought together some of the top experts in sports medicine. In the House of Commons in December 1983, the College was praised as being one of the world's foremost accredited centres for drug control.

The important work being done in Chelsea has been given a greater significance in the eyes of many athletes because it has the financial support of the Sports Council and also the backing of leading figures in the athletics world including Arthur Gold, president of the Amateur Athletic Association.

In supporting the clinic, a number of MPs in the House of Commons have led the call for stricter control and greater punishments for those taking drugs to boost performances.

Colin Moynihan, a Conservative MP, has suggested that the finding of a banned drug or one of its major metabolites in the body fluid of a sportsman should constitute an offence and that the offender should be punished by a ban for life . . . Only recently the International Amateur Athletics Foundation increased the ban for those found to be using drugs from twelve months to eighteen months.

Colin Moynihan's attitude is uncompromising:

> There could be no mitigating circumstances save where drugs were prescribed on strictly medical grounds. Those cases should be referred to an appeals procedure controlled by each governing body.
>
> In Britain, we should substantially extend the present system of random testing analysis and detection, making sure that tests are implemented not just at major events.

The Government's view is a strong one. What is now planned is an amendment to the controlling Medicines Act in an effort to prevent sportsmen bringing prescription-only medicines into the country for their own use.

Sports Minister Neil Macfarlane said it was significant that in Britain the bid to control and restrict the use of drugs had the support of such bodies as the Sports Council, who wanted to eliminate it and to catch the people who were still distributing drugs to athletes on a random basis.

The Sports Council's situation is significant. Its support for the Chelsea drug centre for the twelve months up to the end of 1983 was £100,000, and that did not include their open ended contribution towards the costs of individual tests.

The Council's view is that it will support the search for ways to detect the use of drugs and will encourage as wide a range of bodies as possible to seek out people who are taking them. It encourages those such to send individual tests to the centre, where methods of detection are becoming more sophisticated. The not-so-good news is that in 1983 only fourteen governing bodies made use of the facilities which are acknowledged as being the most advanced in the world. The number of tests carried out was just 800 – a figure described by Neil Macfarlane in the Commons as being 'frankly disappointing'. He commented:

> The drug centre has the ability and the methods to end the abuse of drugs. The Government is taking action to close one of the existing loopholes which permits athletes to bring medicines into this country for their own use as long as they do not forward purchases to third parties. But there is only so much that it will do. The lead has been made by the Sports Council

and has the support of the various bodies. What is not happening, I believe, is that there is not enough day-to-day policing of standards inside some of those specific sporting bodies.

There is little dispute about this. The Chelsea clinic has provided the climate for the much stricter control of drugs in this country. The administration and framework are there. What the government is now doing is monitoring the number of bodies making use of the centre and seeking to develop the unit to handle additional drug testing cases at minimal costs.

Anabolic steroids were used for the first time after the end of the Second World War, to build up concentration camp victims. The weight gain using this specific form of drugs can be enormous. Behind the Iron Curtain some shot-putters are claimed to put on five stone in six months in this way.

The situation is a constant headache for the various controlling athletics organisations. Many, including the International Olympic Committee, have confessed their inability to stamp out the use of the steroids.

Professor Beckett was Britain's representative on the Medical Commission of the International Olympic Committee which has considered the way to control drugs. At the Mexico Games the use of drugs was significant. By 1972 and the Munich Olympics it was so widespread that it was literally beyond control.

Drugs were freely used at Munich – by athletes competing in the shot, discus, javelin, pole vault, decathlon and many other events, especially weight-lifting.

The outcome of the Munich experience was a message to the administrators – if you cannot find a test which proves the use of the drug, then it will not be possible in the future to put a ban into effect.

That was twelve years ago.

I covered the 1972 Olympic Games as a journalist, spending three weeks in Munich. In the eyes of many of the administrators and commentators the use of drugs at those Games had already turned the sport into a farce. Drugs of all descriptions were readily available – and used. This involved far more than the steroids – drugs to aid recovery and so-called 'pep-pills' were in common use as well.

A number of the Munich administrators were concerned

because of the lack of threat to the athletes. There was random testing; small and insignificant a number of blood, urine and sweat tests were carried out. Positive results were found and some Iron Curtain athletes, specifically some from East Germany, were banned under the weight of as much publicity as could be brought to bear.

But it was hardly a scratch on the surface.

Since then, the testing has been modified and the Chelsea drug clinic keeps confidential both its methods and ability to detect the long-term use of drugs. There have been significant moves forward – enough for many to believe that athletes are now much more wary about how and when they use drugs.

The emphasis has been put on explaining to athletes the long-term dangers and consequences of drug abuse.

The less glamorous side of the use of drugs is well documented. It includes former athletes who have suffered from heart attacks, general heart problems and widespread liver and kidney damage. A team of doctors has reported that the use of such drugs could be a factor in the cause of cancer of the liver. There have been other cases of athletes suffering from an abrupt end to their sex lives.

The build-up to the Los Angeles Olympics has seen a fresh international call for the level of punishment to be stepped up. The situation still exists that whereas an athlete who seeks to over-claim expenses at an amateur meeting faces a ban from international athletics, a drug offender can be back in competition within eighteen months.

A central problem is that many governing bodies in athletics are actually the agents of the drug-taking programme. The suggestion has been consistently made that in East Germany and other Iron Curtain countries drugs are offered to athletes as part of the national programme. Drug-taking is not a matter of personal choice as in the West – but almost policy.

The attitude of the athletes in Britain and in America has been simple. Most of those who lead the world rankings are using drugs. In the past it has been quite impossible to compete in the same league unless one gets up to the same tricks.

As one javelin thrower admitted:

When I joined the international field we would go abroad and compete and get beaten not by a few feet but by 20ft and 30ft. They were in a different class. You are faced with a choice – you take drugs and compete or you don't bother.

The most dramatic effects of anabolic steroids have been seen in some of the female competitors, again mainly from Eastern bloc countries. As one senior British coach said:

They can become more like men. They are making a sacrifice. They are saying they will abuse their bodies and change their physique. And using drugs, they can. They can lose curves and their voice becomes deeper, they develop hairs where they shouldn't and of course their muscular development is frightening.

I think a number of athletes in this country have become convinced that a controlled use of steroids may be safe. They see it as giving them a boost in training. They're also aware of the tricks of the trade – specially using the diuretics to 'wash out' the effects afterwards. The mistake which has been made is to test at competition stage. It's too late then. You can go along to a track meeting in this country and see people who will freely give out the pills to athletes as an incentive to become more attracted to the sport.

You get to know the people who carry the drugs. I don't think they are evil; they carry them because they believe especially young athletes, who have a job to go to, need the incentive to make the most of the training programmes.

So is there any evidence that athletes are not taking the drugs in such large numbers?

In 1976 in Montreal, compulsory spot checking for drugs was introduced for the first time and fifty random urine samples were taken every day. This was a step introduced after the system was abused in Munich.

Four years ago the screws were tightened even further at the Moscow Games, where urine tests were common with random tests on up to a hundred athletes.

In Los Angeles the International Olympic Committee promises the most stringent action in the history of the Olympic Games. It intends that every athlete attending the Games will be officially warned of the testing processes and of the anti-drug policing to be employed.

New equipment tested in New York which can detect drug

31

samples with three times the accuracy of tests employed at previous Olympics will be used, but the main message of the IOC's medical commission is to prevent and not to detect.

Through each country's Olympic organising committee, the effort has been made to deter. What many British athletes fear is that the warnings and all the other considerable efforts being made will fall on deaf ears so far as Iron Curtain countries are concerned.

One senior member of the British squad admitted that drugs had not disappeared from the scene.

You can get them easily, but that's not the problem. It isn't illegal. What I've been aware of is that there's been a change. I think a lot are worried about being caught out. Some of the distance runners will be using amphetamines, I'm sure of that, but it is a risk. You've got to remember that most athletes will try things out to see what happens. I think a lot have been scared off about drugs and want something different.

Peak performance . . . with amino acids

Forty six top United States athletes – each one of them considered to be an Olympic medal hopeful – began a unique experiment in July 1983.

For six months they tested performance levels using a natural alternative to anabolic steroids called amino acids.

In December the results showed that 92 per cent had improved on their previous personal best times or performances. The details of the programme showed that the athletes, including some of the best in the world, such as world record holder for 1500-metres Mary Decker, world record discus-thrower Mac Wilkens, world shotput champion Brian Oldfield and many others, had gained in many departments of their body potential.

They had been able to increase endurance while at the same time avoid some of the dangerous side effects of the drug approach, such as damage to blood-sugar levels, to hormone balance and to the liver.

Dr Vic Evans said after the tests:

We have found a natural alternative to steroids which will allow the athlete to make better use of his body. Amino acids will out-perform anabolic steroids over the long term and do so without any of the debilitating or life-threatening side effects inherent to steroid usage.

Such is the enthusiasm for the discovery of the value of extra amino acids that a much more detailed research programme is now being started in the United States, involving over two hundred athletes including sprinters, wrestlers, baseball and basketball players and weight-lifters.

Amino acids are the basic components of protein and the

33

body's primary source of nitrogen. The body's single most important nutrient, amino acids have become known as the building blocks of life and are responsible for all tissue and cell growth, also repair.

In fact, between 10 and 15 per cent of the calories we eat come from proteins which are compounds of carbon, hydrogen, oxygen and nitrogen. They are structures made up of an 'alphabet' of twenty or so amino acids, which are arranged in the body in a complex system. Some of these essential amino acids can be manufactured by the body itself, but there are eight which it cannot make and these have to be found from other sources.

The 'essential' amino acids (see Appendix 4) are isoleucine, leucine, lysine, methionine, phenylalanine, threonine, tryptophan, serine and valine. They are essential because they are responsible for much more than cell, tissue and muscle growth. They play a key role in the manufacturing of enzymes, antibodies and certain hormones, and are needed for the structure of hair, skin nails and bone tissue.

Without them, life would cease.

The amino acids can be obtained from a balanced diet, but for the athlete that would require the intake of far more protein than is necessary, involving excessive calories as well as valuable time and expense. Early trials with the natural amino acids, taken in tablet form, could lead to improvements in the many functions they regulate – such as moods, memory, use of oxygen, blood sugar, iron levels, endurance, energy and the burning of fatty acids.

A report in the *New England Journal of Medicine* on tests carried out in Washington University Hospital in 1982, found that the use of amino acids in supplement form had considerable effects in relieving stress and giving greater energy to patients recovering from major illness.

The report noted that the provision of such amino acids accelerated the repair of damaged tissue and added new muscle tissue for greater strength. One of the most significant effects was that it caused changes in the body without any damage to blood sugar levels or fluid retention. Such damage to the body is a matter of course with anabolic steroids.

The latest tests on US athletes took into account their different needs. While some were seeking added muscle-mass and strength, others had a priority for endurance and reduced body fat. The

34

success of the natural approach with amino acids was accepted by medical researchers and coaches.

Don Hood, head coach of the Albene University team which took part in some of the trials, said:

> I put several of my best athletes on the amino acid programme and without exception they agreed that it gave them a real boost in their performance and physical well-being. The weight men and vaulters all experienced strength gains and the runners felt stronger and more fit during both work-outs and competition.

Recent research has shown that athletes have substantially higher protein requirements. One of the reasons for investigations into whether extra amino acids could help performances, was the belief that often dietary protein was not providing the right levels of the essential substances. Since the digestive process needs time and energy to break down the protein there would be a significant loss in amino acids, the effect of such a loss being to harm the body.

This would mean it was difficult to maintain sufficient nitrogen balance, which is critical for an athlete for muscle growth, extra strength and better endurance and recovery times. As amino acids were known to be essential for the body's supply of nitrogen, then they were seen as important to the diet of athletes or anyone involved in sport.

Amino acid supplements are concentrated, natural, and safe to use.

Many United States athletes began to be enthusiastic about amino acids in the late 1970s because they provided a safer alternative to anabolic steroids which were becoming subject to more and more public attention and criticism.

A comparison between the use of amino acids and anabolic steroids shows the benefits. Bill Kazmaier, world champion weight-lifter, made the change-over to the natural approach to finding something extra in performance terms. He was encouraged to do so after experiencing considerable side effects with drugs.

> My workouts are faster and more productive. I am now stronger than ever at the same body weight – and that is very

important. The use of amino acids as a safe drug-free approach has got to be applauded by the serious athlete.

Bob Rohde, senior coach at the University of Minnesota, added his views:

> Since we started using amino acids, the athletes have maintained a higher performance level, recuperative powers are much faster and I think the mental attitude of the athletes has improved a lot.

American athletes involved in the trial considered the amino acids to be the most effective part of their diet. The success story influenced athletes in Britain and other parts of Europe who were encouraged by its success and reputation.

As part of the Olympic build-up, French weight-lifting athletes and swimmers have been carrying out trials using extra amino acids supplied in supplement form. In Sweden, amino acids have been given to every member of the national squad training for the Los Angeles Games.

Medical research has shown that if they are taken as part of a balanced diet, many amino acids can be poorly absorbed and not effective. In 1982, a research programme found that amino acids supplied in supplement form meant that active people were absorbing nitrogen 16 times greater than that from foods which were rich in amino acids.

When the nitrogen intake is equal to the amount of nitrogen lost through urine or perspiration, the body is said to be in 'nitrogen balance' and the protein from the diet is enough to replace and repair tissue. In that state there is no room for extra performance from the body. When you take more nitrogen, the positive effect means there is literally room for things to improve. The body has extra potential by means of the extra nitrogen – and it also has greater potential to repair damaged tissues.

Said Dr Donald Myerson from the California Research Institute:

> Amino acids will not increase muscle size unless you use them for that purpose and train accordingly. As a runner amino acids will definitely enhance your recovery time and reduce muscle soreness, as well as improve your energy and endurance levels

through better oxygen and fatty acid utilization. Amino acids also delay the onset of fatigue through the rapid removal of ammonia from the blood.

It has been recently shown that amino acids make a significant contribution to energy, particularly leucine and alanine. Other effects that occur from the use of amino acids are improved concentration, faster healing and reduced body fat levels which can improve your performance.

There is a clear advantage over anabolic steroids which are dangerous, although not illegal, as far as the full-time athlete is concerned. Anabolic steroids do not build body muscle – they retain nitrogen and accelerate protein synthesis, but only amino acids deliver nitrogen and build muscle.

There is little doubt that size and strength increases when using steroids. Then they are powerful drugs. These size and strength gains are due to the retention of fluid in the muscle cell, which can mean a bloated appearance.

Dr Myerson mentioned also that as soon as athletes stop taking the steroids there is a rapid and dramatic loss in muscle size, in some cases as much as 30–50 pounds:

Steroids have dangerous side effects which no athlete should be in doubt about. They encourage a fat build-up that can lead to kidney, liver and heart malfunction as well as aggressive behaviour and the inability to produce the male hormone – testerone.

One United States company – Unipro from California – has funded a huge research programme into amino acids. The company was started by a group of research scientists who saw the potential of amino acids, not only for athletes seeking to add to their already high performance levels but also for the weekend sportsman.

They recommend that for the best results amino acids should always be taken at least forty-five minutes before a meal of other protein. It is also important to make sure there is enough carbohydrate intake before training to meet energy demands, leaving the amino acids to work in protein synthesis.

The effects are quick. Most athletes reported an effect within twenty-four hours, in terms of increased energy and faster recovery rates. The longer-term benefits – up to twenty-one days – include reduced body fat, improved muscle tone firmness and increased strength.

Perhaps the last word about amino acids, which have now been seen as a significant factor in the move towards the higher performance level of the natural athlete, belongs to Gary Armstrong – one of the United States' top four decathletes who was one of the first Olympic squad members to try them out in a long-term trial:

> In the months since I started taking amino acids I produced my best ever set of times and performances in almost every one of the ten disciplines. I feel quicker, more powerful and one of the most important things to me personally, is I seem to be able to recover quicker from intense work-outs. I have seen a very good response.

The evidence clearly indicates that athletes have proved that taking concentrated amino acids alongside a diet supplying plenty of unrefined carbohydrates provides a powerful combination.

The high performance vegetarian athlete

A nutritional study of 120 athletes in 1981 found that one of the priorities for their diet was meat, meat and more meat. They claimed it was important as a source of the protein which was so vital to their being able to train and perform.

The high protein theory is a myth, which athletes would do well to leave behind.

A much more sensible step and one with proven results of success is to axe meat altogether. In this case the immediate concern would be that an athlete might not be getting enough protein.

However, a vegetarian athlete can get sufficient protein from wholegrains and from a wide range of foods, without eating meat which in any case is full of unhealthy cholesterol and unsaturated fats.

United States nutritionist Nancy Clark, who has worked with many top athletes in the past ten years, says:

> The vegetarian athlete can easily eat all the protein he or she needs, as well as all of the vitamins and minerals, by eating a variety of foods. Sometimes vegetarians don't get enough iron and zinc but that isn't a major problem. The benefits are enormous by cutting out the sort of high fat products which are destined to damage an athlete's body. It means that it isn't possible to reach those higher performance levels.

Nancy advocates a simple three-point plan for an athlete:

- Have smaller portions of meat and larger portions of starches and vegetables. Cut down gradually but decisively on the meat you eat. Switch to lean white meat as a first move

- Make more casseroles with rice and pasta. Aim at two or three meatless meals a week
- Learn to be more imaginative and creative about your food. Cutting out meat from your diet does not mean your food will be bland or boring. In fact it's exactly the incentive most people need to bring more imagination to their food.

The vegetarian approach is now being taken very seriously and it's no longer rejected as being cranky.

Only during the past three or four years have athletes, their coaches and the people who prepare the diets for them been prepared to replace the traditional steak and eggs preparation with more fruit, vegetables and alternative forms of protein.

The latest recommendations being made for Olympic athletes, in a diet sheet issued in January 1983 through the Sports Council, stressed that complex unrefined carbohydrates should replace the higher protein food in their diet. This was done in the belief that it would provide better quality, energy and endurance in a wide range of athletes.

The classic and memorable example of the vegetarian runner in the UK is Dr Barbara Moore, whose running exploits in the 1960s won her national fame, as someone who insisted on mainly raw foods as her source of energy.

She raised a question in everyone's mind, for the traditional approach of the athlete has always been 'I need something substantial – salads aren't good enough', followed by adopting a regime based on plenty of steaks.

The trouble was that the high protein philosophy had been accepted from the word go. Shot-putter Geoff Capes led the protein campaign by stressing his own needs for plenty of meat, and it is true that the emphasis of the 'weight' athletes demands that protein should be used to build the muscle power.

However, it all comes down to why the body needs proteins. Since many of the body's cells consist of protein, it needs a steady supply of amino acids to enable it to repair and replace these tissues. There is no way the body can store amino acids, so if you take in more protein than you need the surplus is converted into glucose in the liver and either stored as body fat or simply burnt as a source of energy.

It has been one of the traditional myths about our diet that those who are involved in a lot of exercise or activity need plenty

40

of protein. What athletes in particular need is energy, which as we have already seen can be provided much more efficiently by unrefined carbohydrates.

If an athlete asks how much protein he or she should eat, then the answer is not easy. Most daily intake requirements will depend on a number of factors, but there is little justification for athletes to be including as much as 200g of protein in their diet every day.

The argument which athletes are still refusing to see is that one sort of protein is much better than another. Some proteins contain all the amino acids in roughly the right proportions and this is mostly true of animal protein – meat, fish, milk, cheese, eggs and so on. For this reason there was always a common belief that such proteins were much superior to vegetable proteins. This is not true in practice, however.

Different vegetable sources are low on different essential amino acids. Mix them suitably and you end up with a nutritious meal which is as high as an animal protein meal. Beans complement fibre in exactly this way.

Meat and animal fats are high in fat content, so if you eat too much then your fat intake will become too high to be healthy. More important, it will be too high for you to perform to the peak of your natural ability.

The new criteria which athletes need to adopt indicate that it is not necessary to eat a lot of meat, which in any case also tends to be much more expensive as a major part of one's diet.

If you take in too high a proportion of your calories in meat, then either you will have to cut back on carbohydrates, which is highly undesirable, or you will take in too many calories overall and end up with too much weight.

It makes a great deal more sense to get as much protein as you can from low-fat sources such as white fish, grains, pulses, low-fat dairy produce, wholemeal bread, rice and potatoes.

There is evidence for the disbelieving athlete that such a regime works. American physiologists Irving Fischer and Russell Chittenden, in a famous series of tests, decided to find out the type of diet which would be needed to bring about higher levels of energy and endurance. The results were significant; they showed that athletes can train towards and achieve much higher levels from their body on a protein diet which consisted of up to 50g a day. This is particularly interesting in view of the fact that some athletes have a target of almost 200g a day or even more. In these tests, fitness was also shown to have improved still further in the test groups which cut back their protein intake even more.

Nor did the tests end there. Russell Chittenden, working with athletes at Yale University, found that over long test periods energy levels kept on increasing. As the body became more used to handling unrefined carbohydrates, so it became more efficient.

In the United States a band of nutritionists advocated this approach. Men like Don Banyll, Jean Mayer, Paul Anderson and others tried to get the message through to the new generation of American athletes that high protein just wasn't necessary.

Their efforts were for the most part wasted, however. Training diets continued to stress the need for more protein, more meat, more steaks. The irony for the present-day athlete is that although the message is only now beginning to get through, it has been established as fact for over eighty years.

In tests at Loughborough College and Edinburgh University it has been found that more raw foods and less high fat foods in the diet have produced performance improvements of more than 5 per cent. The reasons are that a low protein diet which is low in fats leaves the body in a healthier state. It has to perform better. Too much fat only deprives the tissues of oxygen and too much protein exhausts the body's mineral reserves and creates a superfluity of toxic waste.

More fresh fruit and vegetables also increase the potential of the cells and improve the way the oxygen is used. So just as training strengthens your heart and pumps more blood with each heartbeat, so the food you eat helps the absorption and the use of the oxygen in muscle cells.

Advocates of the importance of raw food would also point that such a diet would kill all the body's waste toxins, giving the muscle cells ideal conditions in which to create energy.

For the 1983 World Championships in Helsinki, members of the Swedish team became involved in tests on diet in the build-up to the major event. They were tested on a high raw or all raw diet for three days prior to events.

Both before and after the performance the athletes in sprint, middle distance and throwing events had their blood pressure, heart rate, recovery rate and stress levels monitored. In every single test the evidence was that the athletes who had switched to a vegetarian, mainly raw food diet were in far better condition to

42

perform and in eight of the thirteen cases there were improved times and performances.

Are there any deficiencies as a result of switching to a vegetarian diet? The vitamin B 12 is sometimes lacking through a strict 'no meat and fish' diet, because it is not available in cereals, pulses, nuts and fruit. However, vegetarians who eat cheese and drink milk have nothing to worry about – they will be getting adequate amounts. Nutritionists often recommend supplements of calcium gluconate for some vegetarians, but again most of the calcium in the ordinary diet comes from milk and cheese.

The other mineral concern may be iron. Intakes of iron have been found to be good in vegetarians, although some of the iron from plants is bound up in such a way as to be poorly absorbed compared with iron from animal sources. The body generally adapts to a low iron intake by absorbing more of what is available. Eating foods rich in vitamin C at the same meal helps the absorption of iron.

It should be emphasised that you will inflict no serious deficiencies on your body by becoming a vegetarian or – what is perhaps more practical – cutting down considerably on the amount of meat in your diet. In this way your body will not only reach a state of considerably enhanced well-being, but you will have the opportunity to reach its maximum potential.

The vitamin theory

Nine out of ten top class athletes in Britain are now taking 'pills'. The figure in the United States is probably even higher. Staggering though this may sound, these figures do not signify a massive move to drugs – just the opposite in fact, because the pills in question are safe, natural and legal. The process of persuading the present-day athlete that he or she should seek extra nutrients through vitamin and mineral supplements is now almost complete. It heralds the era of the natural athlete.

But this is not just restricted to Britain, or even to the West. Multi-vitamin and mineral supplements have for many years formed an essential part of the diet of Soviet Olympic athletes. Over the past ten years, East German coaches have used nutrition based on supplements as the foundation of their highly sophisticated and detailed preparations. It is not perhaps totally insignificant that during that time their athletes have dominated the world athletics stage.

However, it is not necessary to be an athlete in order to benefit from supplements, although few benefit from it more dramatically.

All Britain's elite squad members have been put on special supplement programmes. Seb Coe, Daley Thompson, Dave Moorcroft, Fatima Whitbread and Alan Wells have switched to a nutrition programme which would have been laughed at five years ago. Their plan is to combine such supplements with good food in order to maintain their form – and add a bit extra for the major events. Multi-vitamins and minerals, vitamin E, B12, ginseng, pollen and so on are a regular and important part of their schedules, wherever in the world they may be.

In January 1984, every member of the British athletics team which would eventually be selected for the Olympic squad was offered the chance of taking part in vitamin supplement programmes. With very few exceptions they agreed.

While many athletes take drugs and damage their bodies in the long term, a natural and legal alternative has great appeal. And while some remain sceptical others are more than positive. Fatima Whitbread, the current British javelin star, the Commonwealth gold medalist who failed by such a narrow margin to win the 1983 World Championships, is one such enthusiast.

She has been taking multi-vitamins and minerals, vitamin E and pollen as part of a specially designed programme. One month after its commencement, she returned from Spain having achieved a personal best and feeling stronger and more confident.

I wasn't really aware of vitamins until recently. I had my training programme and special needs analysed, and a supplement programme prepared for me. It wouldn't have made any sense at all not to have tried it. I am careful with my diet. It's improved, I've made it improve. I'm impressed by the speed of recovery which I've now got. It also gives you a bit of confidence that it's working when you start turning in personal bests.

Alan Wells, the current Olympic champion from Moscow in 1980, remains one of Britain's few success stories in the glamorous 100 metres and 200 metres sprint events.

The Scot now lives in Guildford, Surrey, close to his nutritional advisor, where supplements are part of his life. Few athletes are so convinced of the value of vitamins for their performance. He admits to relying on the high potency vitamins and minerals, vitamin B-complex, vitamin C, protein drinks, trace elements and energy powders to generate power rapidly:

When you're training twice, perhaps three times a day you are pushing your body further and further. I've been doing it now for a long time. I need extra nutrients to get the maximum out of myself. I have to keep high energy reserves in the muscles and I think that's the value of the protein and energy drinks which I've gone over to. I used to have a lot of injuries. I went through a phase when it seemed I would just be back to full fitness and ready to stretch myself for the first time in weeks and then there would be another setback. It takes longer to recover than it used to even four years ago, but that's where the supplements have helped me.

David Moorcroft, former 500-metre world record holder, used supplements throughout his winter training and recovery programme, spent for the most part in New Zealand. There, a Californian nutrition advisor worked out a supplement programme with amino acids, vitamin E, B-complex, vitamin C and ginseng, designed to bring about a faster, more permanent recovery and increase his performance.

The result? Admits Moorcroft:

It's done wonders. I have recovered faster than I thought. I've trained hard but I've felt strong. It's a new approach for me but it's one I'm not going to turn my back on. I think we haven't had enough help and guidance about nutrition over the past few years. Other countries, especially behind the Iron Curtain, look after their athletes so well that they have been much better catered for in terms of nutrition. It's about time we got more involved in it.

The benefits are more likely to be seen in the future, but the trend of acceptance is there, something which seemed unlikely a few years ago.

One nutrition advisor, Dr David Penn, who has worked with athletes at Loughborough College, said:

Athletes are hard-up in general. If you turn up with a free offer, they'll try it out.

That isn't being unkind to the athletes, it's just being honest. I think many accepted vitamins and took them, not thinking too much about it. The athletes we've been dealing with have all come back and said they think extra vitamins and minerals have helped their performances. They see it as being better catered for. The stories about the Soviet and East German athletes are legend. There's often one nutrition advisor for each Olympic athlete. Before every race everything from pulse to blood pressure is taken for comparison with afterwards. Then there's blood and urine tests to seek out any deficiency ready for the next event. It's Rolls-Royce treatment compared with most of our athletes. They can't all be members of the elite squad.

What is true in Britain today in nutrition terms has probably been true in the United States for the past two years. The supplement approach in America has a more fervent, more dedicated feel about it. But then the people of the United States have always been keen on vitamin pills.

The programme developed by John Orsini, professional coach and nutritional advisor to the United States team, has involved working out supplements for his athletes which really do sound like a nutritional shopping list. The programme includes multi-vitamin, multi-mineral tablets, pre- and post-workout high energy vitamins which include vitamin C, bee pollen, amino acids and octacosanol tablets, mineral sustained release tablets and protein powders as a natural aid in weight gain and loss.

> It's a quality programme that's been formulated with a single-minded purpose. It helps the athletes get the absolute maximum out of every ounce of sweat, every hour of training. The athletes have benefited beyond any doubt. They are concentrated doses of nutrients which the body needs. You don't have to be an athlete to need them, it's just that athletes need them more than anyone else – they're the ones who are punishing their bodies day in and day out.

It is the pushing and the training and very often the breaking down which has forced athletes to think about their diet – and to think about nutrition.

As one senior British athlete said:

> You go out night after night and you push and push. It gets harder and harder, not easier. It's lonely most of the time and you have time to think and you need some help. You get to know your body and your limits very well and when you try something new you get to know quicker than most whether it's working or not.
>
> Athletes do want some help, something to keep them going, and don't kid yourself they also want it to be legal.

The debate as to whether or not we need extra vitamins in our diet continues to and fro. If you eat properly you don't require extra. The natural place to get the vitamins and minerals you need is in food and provided you eat a varied selection and don't rely on over-cooked, over-processed foods, you should do just that.

That is the theory anyway. But an increasing number of scientists, researchers and nutritionists would disagree. A balanced adequate diet is becoming more and more difficult to achieve. It is not just that few people eat as well as they ideally should do – there are also other things working against it.

The food we eat now is more and more processed, hence essential vitamins and minerals are killed off. Pollution and drugs also affect the store of vitamins and minerals in the body. There are special groups of people who need the extra vitamins – not only the young, elderly and pregnant as the Government might suggest.

Anyone who is under stress, recovering from illness, or who makes special demands on their bodies is likely to need more supplements. Athletes fall into such a category. Coaches throughout Britain and the United States have been taught that athletes will not get the most out of their bodies if they are eating junk food. They are convinced now that vitamins, minerals and other supplements will not only give athletes better performances, but also protect them from illness and injury.

The message that better nutrition is the path to achieving records has persuaded many athletes that the new natural approach is worth trying out. Medical evidence that it works has been sparse. The word from the athletes is 'yes'; the word from the researchers is 'maybe'.

It has been accepted now for fifty years that requirements for vitamin B1 (thiamine) increase with high energy expenditure and high carbohydrate intake, both usual in athletics. The vitamin is used all the time with sugar metabolism and so athletes have increased their B1 intake because it reduces the chances of fatigue in high endurance events.

The truth is that while the importance of B1 became accepted soon after the First World War, what was not so well known was that it worked together with other members of the B group of vitamins. Thiamine operates only synergistically with B2, B3 and B12, so there was a false base for the importance of B1.

Nutritionist Dr Michael Colgan, Director of the Colgan Institute of Nutritional Science in San Diego, California says that it is only with the long-term use of supplements that athletes will really benefit. There are short term gains which are worthwhile, but a long-term nutrition plan will bring the athlete to the peak of his potential ability:

> We know now that six months is too short a time to test the effects of supplements. Twelve months is more realistic for the physiological changes to occur that raise an athlete from merely good to first class.

Dr Colgan was one of the first to test performances. From 1975 he started to test the effects of supplements on endurance performance with long-distance runners. Included were details about food and the environment. Using a double blind trial, where athletes are not told whether they were taking vitamins or just dummy tablets, the results showed that marathon runners improved their times by up to 8 minutes 52 seconds. There have been other studies on strength and speed athletes.

> In the course of experiments physiological changes occurred in the athletes. All of the athletes receiving supplements had already low resting heart rates (47–55 beats per minute) but they dropped even further by an average of 9.1 beats per minute. Resting blood pressures of all those on supplements also dropped reliably, although their pressures were at the lower end of the normal range already.
>
> Their cholesterol levels were also lower than average before the study. Over the six months they dropped further for three of the athletes given the vitamin supplements. Other beneficial changes occurred too, but the heart rate, blood pressure and cholesterol level changes are the most clearly beneficial because recent studies show that the top half of what are commonly called the normal ranges are indicative of widespread cardio-vascular diseases.

The trials also helped athletes to prevent injury. Thirty-five per cent had fewer minor injuries and 81 per cent fewer injections.

Adds Dr Colgan:

> Give your body a minimal exercise habit, along with the vitamins and minerals, and it will respond beautifully. Many people have been on our programme of individual supplements now for five to eight years. They are changed men and women.

So where does an athlete start when it comes to deciding what vitamins he or she should take?

Members of Britain's Olympic squad are lucky enough to have had special programmes designed for them. For others it is not so easy.

The B group of vitamins

One of the key groups of vitamins is the B range – B1 (thiamine), B2 (riboflavin), B3 (niacin, niacinamide, nicotinic acid), B5 (pantothenic acid), B6 (pyridoxine, pyridoxol and pyridoxamins), B12 (cobalamins), folic acid (folacin), biotin, choline, inositol and pABA (para-amino-benzoic acid).

Collectively they have been called the energy vitamins and a multi-B complex vitamin is virtually essential for any athlete or indeed anyone who is involved in much activity.

Members of the B group of vitamins are related through their functions in converting the food we eat into the energy we need. Thiamine (B1) is converted into energy through one compound called pyruvic acid. By taking this particular vitamin you are making sure that pyruvic acid is fed into the energy cycle. So if there is a shortage, the acid builds up in the body and high blood levels result. The symptoms of thiamine deficiency are complex, but include easy fatigue, anorexia, nausea, muscle weakness and a number of digestive upsets. These are all symptoms which reflect how the nervous system depends on glucose as its main source of energy.

Thiamine is contained in all animal and plant foods, but there is a wide variation in their content. Cereals, potatoes, nuts, beans and other pulses are the best sources, but there is a difficulty; thiamine loss can come from food, where alkaline baking powder causes up to 50 per cent loss.

Refined carbohydrates also induce a deficiency of the vitamins because the foods have already had their vitamin power removed during processing and refining. Thiamine is essential for a healthy heart. Tests in Canada, New Zealand and more recently in Japan have shown a lack of it causes slow heart beats, enlarged hearts and eventually heart failure. The next member of the B family – vitamin B2 – is essential to cell maintenance and energy metabolism, also for all cell repair after injury.

It is a common story that runs through all of the B vitamins – vitamin B3 deficiency shows itself with muscular weakness, general fatigue and often skin complaints. Vitamin B5 is essential for energy metabolism.

As a rule, if you are short of one B vitamin you are likely to be short of the others too, so the odds are that most people need supplements with extra vitamin B. The needs of athletes are even more critical.

Ginseng

Many athletes have now opted to have ginseng added to their supplement programme – to relieve stress and help in recovery from tiredness. The herb has been included in the training programme of endurance athletes in particular.

Researchers now believe that ginseng prevents tiredness, headaches, exhaustion and amnesia. It is seen as a powerful restorative agent, which has effects that are not limited to any organ or tissue, but are spread throughout the body. Its ability to increase vitality is what makes it so precious and has done so for thousands of years as far as the Chinese are concerned, for they regard vitality as the essence of health.

Ginseng stimulates the nervous system and reflexes have been shown to speed up. Professor Petkov, of the Institute of Advanced Medical Training in Sofia, has been occupied for the last fifteen years with elaborate experiments to assess its effects on the nervous system. He finds a typical stimulation of the brain wave patterns (electroencephelogram) when experimental animals are given ginseng, and has repeatedly observed that the speed of conditioned (learned) behaviour in both animals and human subjects is increased. This implies an increase in efficiency of cerebral activity. Repeated laboratory tests have shown that the active principles of ginseng root are able to prevent fatigue and to increase the physical performance of animals, including man.

But it is for the benefits of relieving stress that most athletes are recommended ginseng. The body has automatic mechanisms which are called upon if a dangerous or potentially harmful situation arises. Loud noises, threats, wounding, fear, anger, emotional tension and so on, all generate the automatic stress response. The response is controlled by hormones. Hormones are chemical substances made in various glands around the body, which control and integrate the body metabolism and co-ordinate the response of the body to the world outside. They are like nerves, but their message is slower; if nerves are the body's telephone system, then hormones would be the postal service. The stress response is governed by hormones secreted from the adrenal glands, just above the kidneys. These hormones produce a state of readiness and mobilisation in the body. Blood is shifted away from 'peacetime' functions, such as digestion, to the muscles. The heart then speeds up, blood vessels contract, blood pressure rises, the metabolism changes, the pattern of body defences against injury and infection alters and the mind becomes aroused.

While occasional stress is often necessary and can help to keep one alert and motivated, too much stress is undoubtedly bad for the body. Whether it is stress from outside – such as experienced by busy administrators or workers in a noisy factory – or from inside, in tense and anxious people, continuous stress is disastrous for health. It lowers resistance to disease and vascular problems, has been implicated in cancer, and is a direct cause of digestive troubles, gastric ulcer, tiredness, insomnia, migraines and other diseases. The body is drained of vitality when its defences are overworked.

The major success of scientific research on ginseng is that it has repeatedly been shown that ginseng helps the body to cope with stress. In laboratories in Korea, Russia, Bulgaria, America and London, mice under stress have been given ginseng. They showed two basic improvements. First, there was an increase in the weight and function of the adrenal glands, together with fewer abnormalities of behaviour and distress: the mice were, in fact, more able to 'absorb' stress. One is reminded of the Chinese soldiers who take ginseng with them to the battlefield to help them resist the effects of stress and shock. Secondly, there was an actual reduction in the long-term stress response and its corresponding harmful effects. The body had increased its resistance. When ginseng was taken, the animals coped better with actual stress but the body activity settled back to normal more quickly.

Vitamin C

Vitamin C is not just a good way to stop getting colds. For the athlete it's a natural way to heal wounds and help the body to recover from illness and damaged tissues.

The secret is how to make the best use of the vitamin. The occasional orange or lemon drink will not do. Vitamin C is not stored in the body and we need at least 45 milligrams a day to stay healthy. The vitamin, in the form of ascorbic acid or cevitamin acid, helps to form collagen in the body which is so important for the growth and repair of body tissues, gums, blood vessels, bones and teeth. It also helps the body to absorb iron.

Any kind of infection increases the body's need for vitamin C, since at these times it disappears completely from the blood and the urine. When large doses of the vitamin are taken, it has been found that many illnesses can become less severe. It is much more than a matter of curing the common cold. Even so an athlete still needs to use vitamin C to give his body an insurance against infections – including colds.

The theory was introduced in America by Nobel prizewinner, Dr Linus Pauling, who maintains that taking around 2 grams of vitamin C per day will reduce both the number of colds and their severity. He recommends that at the first sign of a cold, 500mg should be taken, a dose which is then repeated every few hours while symptoms persist.

Scientists do not yet believe they have established all the functions of vitamin C.

The connective tissue which holds together all the body cells depends upon an ample supply of vitamin C, and when there is a serious deficiency the structure of this tissue breaks down. This leads to blood seeping from the capillaries, giving rise to nose-bleeds, thread veins, bleeding gums and a tendency to bruise easily (all of these are early warning signs that you are short of vitamin C).

At the same time, the bone structure suffers because the minerals calcium and phosphorus can no longer be laid down in the bones, since the collagen (the protein in connective tissues and bone) is too weak to hold them. This means that broken bones will be slow to mend, as will any kind of wound.

Muscles and ligaments become weak too (and may even be paralysed), while teeth become loose, gums become inflamed and anaemia may occur, along with aching joints and limbs.

53

All these symptoms were common enough in the past when scurvy, now known to be a vitamin C deficiency disease, was the scourge of seafaring men. It was many years before it was realised that adding citrus fruits to the diet of men at sea would keep scurvy at bay. The disease is extremely rare these days, and it has been established that a daily intake of vitamin C as low as 25mg is sufficient to prevent its occurrence.

Vitamin C also helps in the absorption of iron, a mineral which the body has difficulty in utilising. At the same time, vitamin C acts as a detoxicant, and as such helps the body to cope with allergies (if taken in sufficient quantities, the vitamin counteracts the harmful effect of allergens in the body). Similarly, it helps the body to repel toxins and assists in mobilising heavy metals like copper, lead and mercury so that they can be excreted.

Vitamin C also helps to combat the dangers of nitrates and nitrites, which are widely used as food preservatives in such foods as cheeses, processed meats and sausages. It does this by preventing the nitrates from combining with other substances in the body to produce cancer-forming nitrosamines.

Vitamin E

Vitamin E has become known as the vitality vitamin and for athletes it is the key providing new channels of blood supply. For several years now coaches have recommended the use of vitamin E to build up and obtain peak performances from muscles.

The operations of the muscles are so complicated that science still does not fully understand them. It is known that muscle makes up 40 per cent of your total weight, and that there are two main types of muscle, voluntary and involuntary.

The voluntary muscles, sometimes called 'skeletal muscles', are used to walk, run, lift heavy loads, support weight on the back or turn the head. Their function is the movement and support of your skeleton. There are about 620 voluntary muscles, each with its own name, nerve supply, function, and points of origin and insertion. They are called striated muscles because, as can be seen under the microscope, they have stripes. In healthy people, the voluntary muscles will shorten or contract on demand.

To every rule there is an exception and the heart muscle is one; under the microscope it is striated, but (except for a few people like yogis) we cannot control its beating. It is therefore called an 'involuntary striated muscle'.

Smooth muscle fibres, on the other hand, are shorter in length and of smaller diameter than striated muscle. These fibres are arranged in sheets rather than bundles. Several sheets may lie on top of each other, but within each sheet all the fibres run in the same direction. The sheets are arranged so that the direction of fibres in one sheet is different from those on the other side. It is the smooth muscles which make up the muscular layers of the intestines, blood vessels and bladder. We have no conscious control over them.

The more unsaturated fats in the diet (or body), the more Vitamin E is needed to prevent the fat harming the body.

Researchers have found that muscle tissue rapidly accumulates polyunsaturated fats. A vitamin E deficient animal may depend not only upon an imbalance within a tissue, but also upon the fact that, after a muscle or nerve cell has lost its reserve of Vitamin E, it may start to perform less well.

Vitamin E deficiency has been found to develop in humans with such conditions as cystic fibrosis, coeliac disease and others which produce a fat.

Athletes more than any others need a sophisticated form of oxygen supply. Vitamin E, supplied in its natural form as supplements, has been proved to provide the right conditions for the muscle to develop.

Muscles require oxygen to function efficiently because oxygen is essential in the conversion of glucose to energy. The only way that oxygen can be supplied to the working parts of the body is via the blood, where it is carried in the red blood cells attached to the red pigment called haemoglobin.

When a muscle is at rest, its oxygen requirements are minimal. As it is called upon to contract to produce movement, more energy is required and so more oxygen has to be supplied. This is achieved by an increase in the blood flow to that muscle. Vitamin E has the ability to decrease the needs of muscles and other tissues for that increased oxygen. In other words, in the presence of adequate vitamin E, the muscle can carry out the same amount of work using less oxygen.

Vitamin E increases the efficiency of oxygen usage by the muscle. Secondly, it helps to protect the muscle against the harmful substances produced when glucose is converted into energy. The importance of the power of vitamin E becomes apparent when we consider what happens when the blood supply to a muscle such as the heart is curtailed.

Arteries are the blood vessels which supply blood – and hence oxygen – to all parts of the body. They can become narrowed for a variety of reasons, including thrombosis (a blood clot), atherosclerosis (thickening of the arterial wall due to deposition of fat) and arteriosclerosis (hardening and constriction of the arteries). Whatever the cause, this narrowing of the blood vessel decreases the blood supply to the heart or other organs. The veins carry oxygen towards the heart and when these become blocked, insufficient blood reaches the heart and stagnation results. In either case the muscles and organs suffer because they are receiving insufficient oxygen.

Vitamin E allows these cells to function efficiently on less oxygen. It conserves the small amount of oxygen that is available and so helps preserve the life and usefulness of those cells. The famous Canadian doctors, the Shute brothers, who pioneered the treatment of heart disease with vitamin E, have taken photographs of organs that are suffering from a decreased blood supply. After treatment with vitamin E, further photographs have clearly indicated a regeneration of the dead area as a result of the conservation of available oxygen produced by the vitamin.

The heart muscle itself is supplied with blood by the coronary arteries. When these become blocked a heart attack is often the result, because of insufficient oxygen supply to that organ. A similar situation can arise in the brain, where a blockage produces a stroke, since the brain is very sensitive to lack of oxygen. In the legs, similar constrictions cause the complaint known as intermittent claudication, where pain is produced on exercise because of lack of oxygen to the leg muscles.

It is also worth noting that vitamin E opens up new channels of blood supply for the athlete. When a blood vessel becomes blocked either totally or partially, the body responds by opening up new blood vessels that bypass the constricted one and thus allow blood to flow to a muscle or organ again. The new system of blood vessels is known as the 'collateral circulation' and vitamin E speeds up its development. This function of the vitamin is important, because a constricted blood supply to any part of the body can result in the 'death' of that particular area.

One of the most important functions of vitamin E is to protect other essential nutrients like vitamin A, vitamin C, vitamin F (the polyunsaturated fatty acids) and the sulphur-containing amino acids. This protective influence takes place not only in the food we eat, but extends to these compounds when they are functioning in the body itself. Vitamin E protects because it is an anti-oxidant — that is, it prevents destruction of these essential components.

Minerals

Multi-mineral supplements providing a balance of the essential minerals have been added to every athlete's training programme by the International Olympic Committee.

Some of us know that if we are anaemic we need iron, and that we ought to have plenty of calcium in the form of milk for strong teeth and bones. But apart from that, little has been known or understood about minerals. But increasingly scientists find out more about the role minerals have to play in our health.

Research at all levels in centres throughout the world has, over the past twenty years, shown that a lack of minerals in the daily diet can be just as serious as a lack of vitamins.

With the entire study of minerals, a vastly complex process, one important factor has emerged time and time again: the importance of some minerals which the body needs in minute quantities — even one millionth of a gram. These have become known as trace elements. Deficiency of these has caused illness, just as serious as those caused by deficiencies of some vitamins and minerals which the body needs in far greater amounts.

The study of trace elements is a new science compared with the steps taken fifty years ago to isolate and identify vitamins from food sources. Vitamins such as A, B complex, C, D, E and K were all discovered between 1926 and 1948.

So if the first half of this century belongs to the discovery of vitamins, then the second half surely will see the growth of knowledge about minerals.

Until this century, only iodine and iron had undergone sufficient tests in laboratories to show that they could combat diseases which went with inadequate diets.

It is only during the past thirty or so years that methods for detecting trace elements have been developed to such a degree as to make us aware how vital they are for our health and long and happy life.

The main source of minerals is the soil and whereas vitamins are brought together or synthesised by plants and animals, minerals must come from outside. That is perhaps why essential elements are still being recognised and the depth and range of knowledge will increase in the years to come.

Minerals cannot be made by the body and so we depend on our food and water intake to give us what we need. Therefore, our source of minerals must be the soil, and while plants need only fifteen minerals for their supply of nutrients, we require fifty or more.

The richness of the soil varies considerably over the surface of the earth – not only in the quantity of the minor mineral trace elements, but even in the major nutrients for any soil – nitrogen, phosphorus and potassium. As the richness of the soil varies, so deficiencies can be found. Leading on from this, where there are soil deficiencies, medical research has found that there is a correlation between such a deficiency and the health – or lack of it – of the people living there.

Large areas of the Mid-West states of the USA are deficient in iodine, a mineral known to be an essential part of some hormones. Iodine deficiency makes the body metabolism slow down and the thyroid gland can become enlarged into a goitre.

Cancers, leukaemia and heart disease can all be related to areas showing mineral deficiencies. A close connection has been found where researchers have related the number of people suffering from these diseases to soil deficiencies in the areas where they occur.

Studies in the Middle East have found a high proportion of dwarfs living there and this has been linked with a low amount of zinc – when the patients were given zinc doses their condition improved.

In certain areas of Asia, eastern USA and Switzerland there is a chromium deficiency in the soil and this has been linked to a high number of heart-related diseases. Selenium is distributed very unevenly throughout the earth's surface, and where it occurs it has been found that the people there lead very active, healthy long lives without trouble from heart disease or cancer.

An ever-growing list shows how we are learning all the time about the effects and importance of minerals. There are now many minerals for which the experts have decided a daily intake

58

requirement. The obstacle here is in working out how much we actually absorb; many foods contain minerals, but fail to be absorbed into the bloodstream.

Our modern lifestyle is not exactly helpful either. Food is over-cooked, frozen and preserved; additives and colourings are put in – all to the eventual loss of vital minerals.

We all need certain amounts of each mineral – the problem is that these amounts differ. There is no set amount you should take – only limits, because too much of a mineral can be as dangerous and harmful as too little.

The main groups of functions for which minerals are needed are: as basic material for bones and teeth, for example calcium, phosphorus and magnesium; and as triggers for enzyme processes in the body processes which are vital to every cell. This is the main purpose of most minerals, but they are also controllers of the balance, amount and composition of body liquids inside and outside our cells.

Use of bee pollen supplements

In 1976 a thousand athletes trained in Finland with a diet low in fat, high in unrefined carbohydrates and with bee pollen supplements.

Bee pollen is the best and most concentrated form to be gathered and produced by bees and while athletes take honey in often considerable amounts many have been unaware of the use of its more sophisticated form. Bee pollen has a very high source of vitamins, minerals and amino acids and has now become part of many training programmes.

Finnish track coach Antti Lananaki said after the use of bee pollen at the 1976 Olympics, 'Our studies show that it significantly improves performance. There have been no negative results since we began supplying it.'

In fact many Finnish runners came away with awards. One of the strongest advocates of the use of bee pollen is Lasse Viren, the Finnish star who won the Olympic 5000 and 10,000 metres at the Munich Olympics in 1972 and repeated the double success in 1976. He takes six to ten tablets a day during training and from four to six during competition.

After his track team had been given bee pollen for four months, trainer Jack Gimmer at St John's University, New York was so convinced of the performance of his athletes that he persuaded the university to start a major research programme, using sixty athletes including sprinters, swimmers and weight-lifters.

Tom McNab, who has been official national coach to British Olympic athletic teams, has been one of the key figures in ensuring that athletes take a nutrition approach to training and to performance:

> I frequently test food supplements. I ask a number of athletes training under my supervision, give them supplements and then

monitor in detail the performance levels. I was asked to test bee pollen and have to admit to being a bit concerned about it. I asked five athletes training under me to take bee pollen – one pill three times a day. Within a period of twelve months the athletic performance of all the five athletes had substantially improved.

Here are the results:

- A female hurdler aged 28 improved her performance in the 110 metres event by almost a second.
- A senior javelin athlete increased his performances from 210ft to 235ft 6ins.
- A 24-year-old hurdler knocked over a second off his personal best for the 400 metres hurdles.
- A male decathlete improved his performances in virtually all his events.

Added coach Tom McNab:

The main value of bee pollen is not just in its direct effect upon training levels but rather on its apparent effect. The rise in training levels enables more work to be done, more skills to be acquired and more muscle to be developed. The effect of bee pollen is particularly notable in underweight athletes. It's usually presumptious to ascribe improvement to any single factor, but I believe pollen has helped not only in performance terms but in the way illnesses and colds have been reduced.

Such was the success of the trial that bee pollen supplements were made available to all the national squad – with 90 per cent taking advantage of this.

The reason for its success relies on the high content of essential elements, which have earned it the reputation of being a versatile and powerful food. It is no secret that one of the first countries to use it in sporting terms was Russia, where it has been included in training programmes for over thirty years. Western athletes first became aware of its use there through visiting Russian ice-hockey teams.

At the Far East Institute of the Soviet Academy of Science in Vladivostock, much of the pioneer research work on bee pollen has been developed with athletes in mind. One senior researcher reported that pollen was:

> . . . one of the original treasures for nutrition and medicine. It contains very important enzymes for the human organism and no natural approach to improve human performance levels can possibly be considered without it.

Is it all in the mind?

Sport is all about competition. And because of that it is also about stress, anxiety and tension.

The athlete has to prepare his mind in much the same way as he prepares his body for his event. The difference between victory and defeat can be related as much to mental preparation as to ability or fitness.

The same principle applies for the weekend sportsman playing squash or football, as for the international athlete taking part in a major event. The levels of commitment may be considerably different, but achieving the right mental approach can have just as much effect on the performance.

How many of us have been late for a game of squash or tennis, have rushed to get changed, dashed straight out on to the court and then wondered why we did not play very well?

It is all a matter of lack of mental preparation.

If that aspect can be so important for the weekend sportsman, consider the effect it could have on a top class athlete. Competing in any sphere of international sport means pressure and anxiety. The rewards are enormous, the training and preparation intense. So coaches and athletes themselves are now spending more time than ever on the mental side of their preparation.

Gordon Adams, British Amateur Athletic Board national coach has welcomed the move for athletes to learn more about human psychology in helping them to plan for an event:

> The need to prepare the body and the mind has added a new variant to athletic performances. It is something that just cannot be ignored.

More is involved than the individual approach – there is also the team approach. In 1981 and 1982 Tottenham Hotspur, one of the top football sides in the country, employed a specialist company to work with them on the psychological approach to the game.

Mike Varney, the club's physiotherapist, said afterwards:

The course was of immense interest and a great aid to understanding the psychology of top sportspeople. In addition it helped me personally to relax following times of mental stress.

Glenn Hoddle, England international and one of the stars of the London club, was equally enthusiastic:

I feel we are streets ahead in the organisation of our team meetings. Individual players are encouraged to explore and express their ideas.

The course set out to raise team spirit and at the same time improve the way in which the team members communicated with each other. But far more than that was involved. The priority was to prepare the players for their task, and it was unlikely to be considered a success if there were no results to show on the field. Relaxation, visualisation and goal-setting targets were introduced – and used in detail in the long build-up to the FA Cup Final which Tottenham won.

Said club manager Keith Burkinshaw:

It helped us to discover a lot about ourselves when pressure was at its greatest and contributed to our two successive FA Cup victories.

The players themselves felt that learning how to relax and talking about problems and worries gave them the kind of confidence they had found difficult to attain otherwise.

Tottenham's lead in realising the importance of the mental approach has persuaded others to follow – including dance academies, gymnastic teams, physical education colleges and many other clubs, groups and organisations.

The team approach is more complex and relies on a different set of circumstances. For the full-time athlete, the 'part-timer' or the club player, it's all about a personal approach to training, to warming up, to preparations for individual events and to motivation.

Dr Nicholas Lunt, who has trained for five years on the psychological approach to sport, has no doubts about the crucial part mental preparation can play in any athletic performance of almost any standard:

> Too often so much time is spent on the physical preparation of the body, while the mental and emotional preparations are left to chance. What is important is the way an athlete approaches training in a more balanced manner, how he or she wins little personal victories that build up confidence. It's about attitudes to performance, both their own and their competitors. It's about motivation before an important race.
>
> Athletes have got to realise the difference it can make. Thankfully so many of our top coaches have now realised this and are qualified in passing on mental help as well as physical training schedules.

Any kind of training demands will-power. The higher the standard, the greater the demands. Training requires the right mental approach, which is much more than having a target in the future such as winning an Olympic medal.

Psychologists stress the importance of ending any sort of a session with a 'victory'. Never finish on a 'low'. If you are out training on the roads, never stop at a moment of tiredness. If it hurts, stop, rest, and then cover the last fifty yards of the session in style with the head up, crossing an imaginary finishing line in strength. It imparts a sense of success and achievement to the session.

If you end on a low point, the body can pass the message on and the mental approach to the session has then been damaged because there has been no kind of victory.

One of the current themes throughout the psychologists' approach to sport is the setting and achieving of goals.

As one experienced qualified psychologist said:

> Make sure that when you go out training you've got something to aim at. If you are running, then it could be a target distance, if you're training with weights, it could be a target number of lifts. The important thing is to set a goal which you can achieve.

65

Make sure you win, make sure you reach the target. The secret of training isn't as much in the way it prepares your body, it's in the way it prepares your mind.

So the message is to employ sensible targets to your training and build them up in a structured way. You will become accustomed to reaching your target and you will feel better finishing strong.

Most coaches now prepare training routines on these lines for thousands of athletes, because they know that behind every session is the need to motivate and achieve results where no immediate result seems possible.

Pounding through cold, dark streets in the middle of winter needs a level of enthusiasm and commitment that is not easy to maintain – even for athletes who have come to accept training as part of their way of life.

The same kind of positive approach is necessary throughout the training itself.

For instance, what do athletes think about as they live through the pain, stresses and problems of regular training? The message which has been passed on to a team of coaches from the Netherlands, equivalent to our own Sports Council, is that it is simply a case of thinking positive.

For six months in 1983, a team of psychologists worked with coaches in the Netherlands from a cross-section of sports – everything from canoeing to soccer, from marathon running to gymnastics. Their main target was to get the coaches to instill into their athletes the need to use their minds in special ways during training. The method was to ask the athletes to imagine their bodies as lights, and then during the training to concentrate on the strength going into their body as making that light stronger and brighter.

As one coach admitted:

We have neglected the mental attitude in training for too long. The training has to be used mentally and physically. It's important to get the athlete to develop concentration and to concentrate on the positive effect of his body getting better and stronger.

The objective is to sharpen the mental state so as to create a feeling that the mind and body are acting as one. A training programme where the athlete is worried, anxious and has outside pressure is likely to be about 30 per cent as effective as one where he or she is relaxed, able to concentrate and be positive.

So when you are training here are some tips to follow.

- Relax yourself before you start. Sit down for a few minutes, concentrate on what you want to achieve. Set yourself a target.
- Try to shut out other thoughts. Think about the way you are running, your rhythm. If you're lifting weights, then look again for a rhythm.
- Think about your breathing and stay concentrated on it.
- If you find your mind wandering, stop and recover the thought pattern.
- Make sure you always reach your goal. Set yourself a reasonable target, but don't make it too ambitious. It is better to finish well and strongly with a less ambitious target, than to fail on a less realistic one.

How often have you heard athletes from many different sports who have taken part in an international contest admit afterwards, 'I don't know what happened to me – I didn't perform well, I just froze.'

Many experienced athletes seize up with anxiety before important races and fail to perform according to their ability. It is not their physical but their mental preparation which is at fault.

Psychologists often quote the classic example of a sportsman who worries about problems at home when he is running, and about his running problems when he is at home.

The mental strength that many champions possess comes from the discipline of total concentration and the ability to prepare mentally for an event. Natural ability is of course crucial, but the body, mind and emotions do not operate independently and the peak performance from an athlete rarely comes unless the combination of all three is exactly right.

So how do you prepare for a major event?

Tennis superstar Billy Jean King firmly believed in a scientific process of mental rehearsal. She became convinced that by sitting and thinking of herself hitting perfect strokes and using perfect tactics, she would repeat the perfection on court. Long before any big championship the woman who won more Wimbledon titles than anyone else in history would rehearse every detail of her game in her mind. She imagined herself walking on court, warming up, playing winning shots. It was mental rehearsal which determined her reactions just as much as on-court practice. Few could deny her record of success.

The techniques of such a rehearsal are not new. They have been used for over eighty years, but have received little acceptance and it is only recently that research has begun to establish some backing for the beliefs. It is known that carrying out any physical or mental task sends minute electrical impulses up and down the relevant nerve paths. Each repetition helps to lay down a record to which the mind can return.

The techniques need complete concentration in order to create the right sort of vivid pictures, but can be immensely valuable. It is a question of learning to picture yourself and your performance; getting the mind prepared for a high level of performance and expecting the best not in the form of a vague hope, but in the form of a powerful visual image.

At its most sophisticated, this is the type of preparation which people like Billy Jean King have perfected. At its more basic, it is the need to sit down and prepare yourself mentally for the task ahead.

It need not be a long-drawn-out process. What it does demand is peace and quiet and concentration. You will need to think about the training programme you have been through. You will need to think about the sequence of little victories which have accompanied every training session and you will need to plan not the tactics but the preparation.

Most important of all is the necessity to get your mind positive. Part of the secret of achieving that is not to expect too much. Few athletes are 100 per cent convinced that they have done enough training, that they have had the right sort of training, or enough competition. Perhaps they have overtrained? The mind can happily create a thousand things which have gone wrong or which have not been done correctly.

What you must do is shut the door on these doubts and get the right thoughts working for you. This takes time and it takes practise. But it is necessary and it does pay dividends.

Not only does this system work for the athlete preparing for top-flight sport, but perhaps even more importantly, it works for anyone who is competing in sport or who wants to improve his or her performance. And that means millions of us.

So the first step is to learn how to relax and concentrate your mind on the task ahead. Meditation should not convey Eastern mysticism and spiritualism; it's merely a way of helping you to relax, concentrate and in many ways increase your overall mental efficiency.

To be effective, meditation needs something to focus on, a relaxed position, a quiet environment and regular practice. The focal point as far as using meditation in sport is concerned could be the competition to come. Fix your mind on the race or the game or the challenge. A relaxed position can be lying, sitting or reclining as long as no muscular effort is involved. To become good at it, you will need to do it regularly.

The whole process should take at least 15 minutes:

1. Make yourself comfortable.
2. Close your eyes.
3. Relax all your muscles, beginning at the feet and moving up the body to the face. Keep them relaxed by repeating the procedure if necessary. Some people find it helps to tense the muscles before relaxing them. Don't become stressed about the need to relax quickly – let it occur at its own pace.
4. Breathe through your nose and become aware of your breathing. As you breathe out, start to count. Don't alter the speed or pace of your breathing pattern, but let it happen naturally. Keep counting for 10 or 15 minutes. From time to time you will get distractions in the way of 'rebel' or straying thoughts. Don't worry about them, but return to counting.
5. Concentrate on yourself and your need to perform. Let your thoughts be pleasant and positive. You will feel a sense of achievement and also a sense of being relaxed. You will also feel that you have contributed to the preparation of the race or game.

For those who take part in sport at any level drive is essential, but remember that you need regular periods of rest, mentally as well as physically. For many of us, it is more than a question of thinking about work or family problems; it is about being in control of your body rather than the other way round.

Competing in sport is stressful and sooner or later you will react with one or more of the symptoms of stress. Different approaches will clearly work for different people, but the athlete has so many special problems to deal with that he has to learn to control the mental approach to becoming prepared.

He has to achieve that mental approach in order to learn how to deal with distractions. He needs to have the control in order to have the inner peace of mind to concentrate when there is the special distraction of a large crowd or – on a lower level – just other people watching.

The athlete must be able to psyche himself up, to learn to prepare not only the day before but during the last few minutes, to shut himself off and to increase the awareness of physical power while not increasing tension and stress.

He needs to be able to motivate himself time and time again to make the effort when there may be a voice inside which says, 'Why should I bother?' He needs to have the ability to recover mentally as well as physically from the effects of injury, without allowing it to damage any feelings of sharpness.

Such things come with learning the right mental approach.

The strains are considerable. If you let it, the mind can worry about anything from a previous injury which perhaps has not really cleared up, to the fact that your opponent only last week turned in his personal best and is certain to beat you.

Any form of mental preparation will help to ease and push such worries away. Even a technique that is designed to relax your muscles has a calming effect on your mind and is one that helps you to become less anxious.

Athletic coaches now encourage meditation. They describe it as spending more time relaxing and thinking about performances and preparations, but it's the same thing. It's training the mind.

If you still doubted its importance, then consider any national sports development programme. Look at the way the Russian athletes spend weeks working with psychologists and psychiatrists in preparation.

The standard training programmes now have a base support of sports organisations which offer the opportunities to train and practise. The next level is the training system where it is more than just taking part that is involved: it's learning how to perform better by learning skills.

The next stage is the body sciences, the nutrition approach, the effect of injuries. But right at the top come the mind sciences – considered to be so important that in the United States and in Eastern bloc countries, more research money is being pumped into study of the effects that psychologists and psychiatrists have on athletes' performances than in any other area.

So to deny the importance of the right mental attitude to sport is to risk throwing away success. The odds are that if you deny yourself the time and effort to control your mental approach, the hours spent punishing your muscles will have been wasted.

Coping naturally with the pre-menstrual syndrome

The effects of the menstrual cycle can mean the difference between victory and defeat for many women athletes. It is a delicate subject, rarely brought out into the open, but recent research has shown that pre-menstrual tension can have a number of implications for our athletes.

And learning to cope naturally with the effects can, researchers now admit, affect sporting performances.

There is little doubt that the physical symptoms of pre-menstrual tension which include weight gain, headaches, migraine attacks, aches and pains as well as depression, tension and irritability have provided a simple explanation for varying levels of achievement.

Many women have to withdraw from competitions at this time. Others have to live with below-par performances. It is not just a case of different performance levels, but also the effects of the cycle as they make up a regular pattern which affects sporting levels.

For the women suffering from pre-menstrual tension, it may be difficult to decide whether the physical or the psychological symptoms are the worst to cope with. Tension and uncontrollable irritability would be at the top of most lists, since they affect so many aspects of everyday lives. For the athlete who is trying to cope with a normal working life and the need to sustain a training programme, often at critical times, the effect can be devastating.

Most women's weight increases by a couple of pounds for a day or two before a period, so the weight is temporarily at its maximum. That alone can slow down athletic performances. The pain threshold is lowered, the resistance to infection is weakened and there could be migraine, giddiness and fainting. Joints, muscles and back may ache and excess fluid in the brain cells may bring on emotional disturbances.

It is unlikely that any sportswoman would suffer all these symptoms at one given time, but it is rare for a female athlete to be totally free of any of them.

The Women's Amateur Athletic Association takes this particular problem into account, their official line being:

> We take it into account when we select international teams and analyse individual performances. If we know a girl was handicapped by this problem in any way, then it seems reasonable for us to discount that result as being out of the ordinary.

Some international athletes use the contraceptive pill to bring on or postpone the regularity of their cycle at the time of important competitions. Doctors advise strongly against this however. They consider it to be harmful and that it can lower performances. Eastern bloc countries are known to take their own way out of the problem and here the use of testerone (the male hormone) to totally suppress menstruation is widespread. This has two benefits for women competitors: it postpones any effect of the monthly cycle and at the same time builds up male muscle formations.

In Britain the Women's Amateur Athletic Association condemns the practice.

The most significant development in helping women to combine training and athletic performances and lessen the effect of pre-menstrual tension has come in a natural product based on the oil of evening primrose. A large number of athletes are involved in trials using the oil to counter the greatest threat — apart from injuries — to their ability to perform well.

The definition of pre-menstrual tension is centred on a group of physical and mental changes which begin anything between two and fourteen days before menstruation and which are relieved almost immediately the period starts.

Thousands of women suffer from it, but it can pose special problems for the sportswoman. Racing can make the athlete physically sick, and there's also a definite loss of co-ordination. A rise in intra-ocular pressure means that excess fluid presses on delicate structures within the eyeballs; this can easily have a physical effect on a woman's eyesight.

She finds it difficult to make the same judgements on distances, and her balance and running rhythm can be affected.

What the female athlete is trying to counter in the best way possible is a series of chemical changes to her body over which she has no control. These are changes which are serious enough for any woman whether she is out at work or working in the home. For an athlete who is training her body to high levels, the effect can be shattering.

Drugs are not the solution. But now the effects of vitamin B6 and oil of evening primrose are giving renewed hope that symptoms can be controlled naturally.

Recent research has shown that a deficiency of essential fatty acids is the basic defect underlying the pre-menstrual syndrome. Essential fatty acids can be compared with vitamins; they are sometimes known as vitamin F and are substances which cannot be made by the body but must be taken in with food. Animals who are totally deprived of essential fatty acids develop many serious problems; they cannot resist infection, they have bad skin and their hair falls out, they develop painful joints and become lethargic and irritable.

By far the most important of these essential fatty acids is linoleic acid. Researchers found that such problems could be corrected by replacing the essential fatty acid back in the diet. Most diets contain no more than one per cent of total calories as linoleic acid, and for this reason few people thought that essential fatty acid deficiency might be common.

There was, however, a major flaw in this reasoning.

Linoleic acid itself is almost inert as an essential fatty acid and is useless if it cannot be activated or triggered into action and converted into substances of vital importance chemically. We need linoleic acid, but only to start the process. That process is complicated, but unless the acid is converted into a substance called gammalinoleic acid (GLA) then it is worthless.

One of the most exciting discoveries in the past ten years has concerned the factors which block the formation of GLA – including such things as a diet rich in saturated fats, diabetes, viral infections and the ageing process.

The benefit of evening primrose oil is to provide the necessary GLA.

Evening primrose oil has been studied in laboratories all over the world, where its remarkable properties are being analysed.

The most significant benefit has been that women taking the oil in supplement form reported dramatic relief from pre-menstrual tension. The effects it had on relieving the physical and mental symptoms have been confirmed by studies at major centres for pre-menstrual studies.

An analysis of clinical trials and research show that it is of assistance to nine out of ten women with pre-menstrual symptoms. It has a very high success rate.

There are two major points in its favour. First, it corrects the essential fatty acid deficiency at source by supplying what the body needs.

Second, it is a natural food product and not a synthetic drug. It can be used in absolute safety and with confidence.

The best way to take it is to use supplements of the evening primrose oil. All the major clinical trials and research work have been based on a product called Efamol. Two 500mg capsules of Efamol should be taken three times a day throughout the menstrual cycle, dropping to one capsule two or three times a day after two months.

The other major success in the control of pre-menstrual tension has been vitamin B6 (pyridoxine), another natural and drug-free alternative which is safe and effective. It has had major successes in clinical trials, most significantly in St Thomas's Hospital in London, and in particular can help to relieve pre-menstrual headache and depression. The usual recommended dose is 40mg of the vitamin twice a day, rising to 75mg twice a day if necessary. It is important to start the treatment three days before the expected commencement of any symptoms in order to derive maximum benefit from it.

Vitamin B6 is obtainable as a supplement, but it is available through foods such as yeast and liver, fresh fish, bananas, prunes and raisins, peanuts, walnuts and whole grain cereals.

The important thing about both vitamin B6 and the oil of evening primrose supplements is that it offers the sportswoman a natural way to control the pre-menstrual effects on her body.

Pre-menstrual tension which is especially severe in adolescence is seen by many doctors as creating a barrier which cuts off many girls from sporting activity at school. They are not sufficiently able to cope with its problems and hence shun any kind of physical activity.

The menstrual cycle gives a woman athlete the sort of potential changes in her performance levels with which it is difficult for many athletes to come to terms. One study which has probed the peaks and troughs of performance levels shows that the low spot comes at the start of the period, after the body has been under pressure with three or four days of discomfort, pain, weight gain and often depression. The peak performances come five days after the start of the period and begin to decline again at the ovulation stage, slipping back gradually until the more dramatic decline begins again three or four days before the period starts.

Sporting bodies are now prepared to bring out into the open what many have clearly thought to be too delicate a subject – that the effects of pre-menstrual tension have to be accounted for in athletic performances.

This is not restricted to any sport, but rather applies generally to all women involved in top level and even club level sporting action. What organisations have accepted is that women need to be given help and guidance in doing everything they can to lessen the effects of such dramatic changes on their systems.

The development and success of the means of coping with pre-menstrual tension naturally with drug-free products has added a new dimension to the ability of the sportswoman to maintain a much higher level of performance.

Should you load up with carbohydrates?

On his way to becoming European and Commonwealth champion, Ron Hill began to raise a few eyebrows.

This was not because of his attitude, his training schedule or his running tactics. What many of his colleagues were not prepared for was the way he promoted the importance of diet in the build-up for an event. In fact, Ron Hill was one of the first long-distance runners to examine his diet closely and become convinced of the benefits of what is now known as carbohydrate loading.

By eating a balanced diet during early training periods and then switching to meals high in carbohydrates when the training is at its peak, the body's glycogen (energy) stores can be greatly increased.

This is one of the most significant ways in which diet can be turned into energy and power. It is a regime which has scientific support and over the past ten years has become a key aspect of the way researchers are learning more about human endurance levels.

Carbohydrates have a bad image in the diet. They have become linked with fattening foods and when people go on a diet, one of the first things they cut out is carbohydrate foods.

In fact an analysis of the energy or calorie content of the pure nutrients shows that fat and alcohol are the richest sources and so the most fattening.

The food we eat has to provide the fuel or energy for our day-to-day lives. That energy is measured in calories. The average man needs roughly 3000 calories a day, the average woman slightly less—2200 a day.

Two-thirds of this energy goes into maintaining the heartbeat, keeping the lungs breathing and the rest of the body ticking over. The remaining third is used for growth and movement. The work of keeping the body ticking over is called the resting metabolism.

Children have a much faster metabolism rate than adults and so they need that much more energy to stay alive. The opposite is true with very fat people; their bodies become adapted to using as little energy as possible and so they have a slower metabolic rate.

Food also provides the body with protein, vitamins and minerals. If the body is unable to get enough energy from food or from the stores of body fat, then it converts protein into energy.

What marathon and long-distance runners are able to take advantage of is the exact converse of this. By eating more than the body needs, the surplus—whether it's protein, fat or carbohydrate—is either burnt off as heat or converted into fat and stored.

The athlete's training programme means that all the extra is burnt off through energy and very little is stored. By opting for carbohydrates to provide that extra food the athlete is being given a considerable reserve of energy which either goes into the training programme or is used in the performance or marathon run itself.

Runners can vary in the way the loading system is used. It can be restricted to a week, where the programme could be:

- Sunday: Rigorous training routine (evening)
- Monday, Tuesday and Wednesday: Low carbohydrate diet —using more fats and protein—and lighter training
- Thursday and Friday: Switch to high carbohydrate diet and easy training
- Saturday: Step up the carbohydrate rate even further and rest
- Sunday: Race

A number of athletes prefer to adopt the same principle but adapt it to a much longer build-up of perhaps three weeks. A tough training weekend would then be followed by a low carbohydrate diet for several days. Training would continue, but on a much lower level. The diet would then be switched to more carbohydrates, with a gradual build-up over four or five days. The training still is not quite so intense. Training stops the day before the race, when the body will have full reserves of carbohydrates ready to be put into action the following day.

Carbohydrate loading in itself is not new. What is new is the research to prove that it works and works efficiently. For the past two years, members of the United States Olympic marathon team have been carrying out tests by using different levels of carbohydrate and analysing performances.

Nutritional advisor Ray Cassio says:

> We've been working on the theory that with hard training, you repeatedly deplete your glycogen stores and then re-load them when you eat. Depletion of those stores at certain times in a training programme can be turned to good effect. The 'starved' muscles super-saturate themselves above the initial glycogen level and you've got lift off.

He stressed that for two years the training programme of many of the United States Olympic team has taken diet into account 'more than ever before'. He added:

> The results are not complete, but what we've found is that over a ten-mile distance, carbohydrate loading has been making the difference of between 3 and 14 minutes. The average is about 6 minutes. That's fifteen minutes off a marathon run. Those figures are comparing athlete for athlete and varying a normal mixed diet with high carbohydrate diets. We have a team of scientists working with us to look at levels.

The benefits now being reaped from such a diet in the United States and in Britain were first developed in the 1960s, although studies can be traced back as long as 45 years ago. The relationship between carbohydrate, the energy stores of the muscles and endurance levels was studied by Scandinavian scientists Bergstrom, Hultman, Hermansen and Saltin, who always believed the link could have a significant effect on the way the body operates.

The starting point was simple. If you exercised hard or were involved in strenuous work, then the amount of carbohydrates in your muscles would drop.

What they worked on was the idea that by eating carbo-hydrate-rich foods for several days afterwards, the muscle glycogen stores would be more than just topped up to former levels – they would be overfull. This build-up of extra energy could be even more effective if a low carbohydrate diet was eaten before the switch to the carbohydrate rich foods.

The scientists found that the ability to perform on exercise machines was directly related to the size of the glycogen stores. By

79

altering the diets, they obtained some inspiring and rewarding results. Everyone who took part in the trial improved their performances, the percentage improvement varying from 1 to 118 per cent. The effect was variable, but effective beyond dispute.

It was not until 1971 that these results were used and adapted. In competition athletes demand an increase in the rate of work in terms of speed and better times. The previous tests had tested duration. What the athlete was interested in was not if carbohydrate loading could make him run further but whether it could make him run faster.

There were of course reports from individual marathon runners who used and believed in the system, which was used in Scandinavia much more than anywhere else in the world. The links between the runners and the scientists and coaches in their own country were strong and there was a commitment to the new diet approach. Significantly Scandinavia began to become a force in distance running.

In 1971 Jan Karlsson and Bengt Saltin reported better running times from a number of 'guinea-pig' athletes who had been put on a high carbohydrate diet. Athletes ran over 30km (19 miles) and the results showed that those who were loaded with carbohydrate consistently outran those on a normal mixed diet.

The times were again variable – anything from 1 to 16 minutes. The percentage improvement, however, was as high as 6 per cent. It was results like this which led Dr Ron Hill, MBE, European and Commonwealth marathon champion with a personal best of 2hrs 09mins 28 seconds, to take the lead in Britain in promoting the use of the diet.

So how does it work?

Bill Rodgers, one of the all-time top marathon runners who long held the world record for the 26-mile run, became a leading figure in the new diet approach in the United States:

I used to run marathons very much with a lot of attention to my diet. I ate high carbohydrate foods for two or three days before the race. I wasn't worried about the extra food because I knew it was a build-up. I was preparing for an endurance event and always thought it made common-sense to fuel up my body. Ever since I began to look at my diet I think there was something extra about the way I was running. I had a feeling of greater strength. Some of my best performances have come after I have used this particular diet approach.

When the body is pushed in long-term exercise, the main supply of energy to muscles is a substance called adenosine triphosphate (ATP), which comes from the carbohydrate and fat stores of the body.

What the athlete must aim for is to ensure that his supply of ATP comes from the carbohydrate rather than the fat stores of the body. Although the amount of energy stored in the body as fat is considerable it is not able to release the supply of energy to the muscles very efficiently. The decision as to what provides the energy giving power to the muscles depends on the store in the body and the intensity of the exercise.

In marathon running, the pace means that ATP comes from the carbohydrate store and will only switch to the less efficient fat store when the carbohydrates have been used up in the glycogen store.

When this changeover happens, there is a cross-over of energy sources which can have a dramatic effect on the athlete. Many of them call it 'running into the wall', and it is a problem time in a race. The effect of carbohydrate loading is to increase the size of the initial glycogen store. If you start with a full tank, then you can go on for much longer.

Carbohydrate loading has its critics. Claims of angina-like pain and damage to skeletal muscle fibres have been made, but are in general unfounded.

Diabetics should consult their dietician before beginning such a regime.

What is required is a common-sense approach. One often quoted story is that of the athlete who ate two loaves of bread at one meal as part of the build-up of carbohydrates, and then complained of stomach pain!

The regime does work and can work for any long-distance runner. The major mistake which is made is in taking the regime to extremes but maintaining a high training programme throughout the diet when there is practically no carbohydrate.

Many athletes who have analysed the effects of this diet approach have been convinced of the physiological advantages.

Apart from energy supply, the other critical problem facing the marathon or long-distance runner is controlling the temperature of his or her body. You can only control it properly with fluids.

In storing the glycogen with extra carbohydrates you also store water, so it helps significantly in offsetting the effects of dehydration. This is a vital factor, because you can maintain the peak performance levels which many athletes are constantly searching for by preventing dehydration.

Extra carbohydrates will not offset it completely, but will play an important part. It is still imperative to take fluids throughout a run.

Loughborough nutritionist Steve Wootton's advice is:

If you do decide to follow the traditional regime, make sure that you plan your food selection carefully. Don't leave anything to chance. If it works for you stick with it. If it hasn't worked for you, take a closer look at your diet.

He believes that athletes should load on carbohydrates on the basis that this could well improve performance time, and that there is a considerable volume of evidence on the importance of having those reserves of carbohydrates to call up during a race.

Diet sheets on carbohydrate loading are now freely available to marathon runners. For the United States squad training for a place in the Olympic team in New England, it has become part of the way of life.

Nutritionist Ray Cassio has made it clear:

Extra carbohydrates doesn't mean a few extra biscuits and plenty of sugar. We've studied diets in great detail and in the build-up to the Olympic trials have stressed the importance of the athletes learning more about their diet for themselves and not relying just on outside help.

One of the key themes has been the importance of not confusing high carbohydrate foods with high fat foods such as ice cream, cakes and pastries. High fat foods have the taste appeal and will fatten you up but they won't fill your muscles with glycogen. Only carbohydrates are readily converted into muscle glycogen.

So how do you go about planning and eating high carbohydrate meals?

What is critical for the athlete is that he or she should concentrate on unrefined carbohydrates – wholemeal bread, cereals, wholemeal pasta, brown rice, fresh and dried fruit – and more use of beans, pulses and vegetables, especially potatoes with their skins left on.

As we have seen, all these should be part of your normal diet. The trick lies in regulating them with a training programme and eating more at certain critical times.

So the message is:

- Eat breakfast—particularly wholegrain cereals and wholemeal toast. Make your own muesli from oats, fresh and/or dried fruits, nuts and natural yoghurt.
- Eat brown rice and wholemeal pasta and leave the skin on potatoes.
- Eat wholemeal bread, snacks and crispbreads.
- Don't throw away the outer leaves of vegetables—they are a richer source of fibre than the inner leaves. Chop them up and use them in soups and stews.
- Eat more pulses. There is a wide variety now available and they can be used as the whole basis of a diet regime—add them to soups, stews and salads.
- Use wholemeal flour in cooking.
- Aim for foods which are high in carbohydrate, yet low in fat and low in sugar.

If you opt for just too much sugar in your bid for extra carbohydrates, it will throw the whole regime out of co-ordination. Sugar and sweet foods in general crowd out more nourishing and less fattening items, and people who eat a lot of them will merely put on weight. If you are working on a carbohydrate loading scheme for one week, too much sugar or sugary foods will make it difficult if not impossible to maintain your appetite throughout the seven days.

So here in detail is a scheme designed to boost performance on the seventh day:

Day One
Exercise: A thorough training programme to use up the body stores of glycogen.

Diet: Low carbohydrate to limit the amount of glycogen being put back into the body. Boiled or poached eggs, cottage cheese, white fish, cold chicken, salads. Don't over-restrict the amount of carbohydrates too soon.

Day Two
Exercise: It's important to keep up a training programme, but at about a half or a third of previous levels.
Diet: Low carbohydrate, still avoiding foods which contain starch or sugar.

Day Three
As day two.

Day Four
Exercise: The training programme is now cut right down. All you need to do is keep the muscles toned. If you are used to running several miles a day, all you now need to do is a steady ten-minute jog and a few exercises.
Diet: A complete change-round with a switch to much more carbohydrates, but remember there are good and bad carbohydrates. Those you need to include in your diet are high in starch.

Day Five
As day four.

Day Six
Exercise: This should be a complete day of rest. Over the week the training schedule should be gradually but carefully reduced further and further. With only twenty-four hours before the race, you need simply to rest.
Diet: You should still maintain normal levels of eating. There is really no need to over-eat. All you are trying to do is eat a balanced diet of the right sort of foods. Teatime is an important meal before the race and you will need a substantial three-course meal. Try soup to start with, using plenty of vegetables. Beans, nuts and pulses should figure in the main dish, with perhaps low-fat yoghurt or a wholemeal pudding or pie. You do not want to wake up on race day feeling bloated. It is possible that over the last three days your weight will have increased. This should be monitored closely, but in any case weighing yourself every day should be part of your routine. If you are perhaps three or four pounds overweight, that is about right.

If you have eaten high carbohydrate foods with plenty of starch instead of plenty of sugar, the extra weight will be to your advantage.
It is advisable to try out the routine in good time. Don't leave

your first attempt at carbohydrate loading until the week before an important race; try it out well before, as there are bound to be personal adjustments you will need to make.

One thing many marathon runners have found is that they need to start building up high carbohydrate into their bodies earlier. Instead of three days of high carbohydrates, sometimes four days are necessary. Always err on the side of caution.

Who benefits from 'loading up'? Marathon runners are a classic example, but it also applies to cross-country runners and long-distance cyclists. It has even been used by people preparing for long weekend walks where there is an extra demand for energy.

In the past few years, carbohydrate loading has become an important part of the natural approach to long-distance running and has been used effectively and with consistent success in performances.

American marathon runner Ron Coote believes that loading with carbohydrates is only possible two or perhaps three times a year:

> I'm sure the body learns that it has been tricked. I've been using it now for several years. I restrict my carbohydrates to purely unrefined ones and I think that is the success behind it. Athletes who have just used any carbohydrates and have filled themselves up with sugary foods haven't had the success with it.
>
> I don't think it's a problem using it three times a year. If I looked at my schedule, then perhaps I'd be looking at three main events when I would want to peak. I'd just use it then.

Research has now established that marathon runners have two or three times the amount of muscle glycogen of the untrained person.

Doctors and nutritionists now believe that laying down the extra glycogen reserves can be done safely and without damage. And now coaches are seeing the proof that it does shave the minutes off performance times to such an extent that it cannot be ignored.

Don't pile on the sugar or the salt

In many athletes' minds there has always been a simple answer to any problems about diet.

Just pile on the sugar! It's got bags of energy and will keep you going.

Or as one senior athlete recently admitted in public: 'If I want a quick energy burst during training, I take along sugar cubes.'

In fact, quick energy is stored in your muscles as glycogen and is readily available for immediate action. If you eat sugary foods for an energy boost, what can happen is that you actually lower your performance levels because you are contributing towards hypoglycaemia – low blood sugar. When combined with exercise, the extra insulin created by the pancreas may cause the blood sugar levels to drop to an abnormally low level; in athletes this has caused a feeling of being light-headed, shaky and uncoordinated.

Boxers are classic examples. They often crash diet to reach a weight target before a fight, and then proceed to eat chocolate bars and cakes in a last-minute effort to regain some of the lost energy. They then become hypoglycaemic and perform badly. It is not necessary to eat sugar for energy. Although simple sugars appear most quickly in your blood – 5–7 minutes after they are eaten – all carbohydrate foods and extra proteins eventually digest into glucose.

Sugar will do more harm than good in your diet and there are two ways in which it certainly does you no good. First, it tempts you to eat too much. Sweet foods crowd out more nourishing and less fattening items and people who eat a lot of them end up by getting fat.

Second, sugar causes tooth decay – a fact which may not put your life at risk but does nevertheless have a significance with respect to your overall well-being.

There are two types of sugar and to the body sugar is sugar

whether it is white, brown, powdered, cubed or granulated.

In whatever form it comes, it will be broken down within the body and either used as a source of energy or stored in the body as fat. Athletes find it difficult to accept that they could get along perfectly well, and in fact a lot better, if they never ate any sugar whatsoever. It provides calories but no nutrients at all and the body can use starch in the same way as sugar. What has happened is that because people like the taste of sweet food, the amount of sugar we eat has shot up as compared with the amount of starch we eat.

The basis for the belief that a sudden 'fix' of sugar will help in the body's performance is that it takes longer for the body to break down a complex structure like starch into glucose than it does to handle a much simpler one like sugar.

What happens if you give someone a spoonful of sugar in the belief that it will provide a lift, is quickly seen. Just as it causes problems to the boxer, the well intended spoonful will leave a sensation of depression and irritation.

The body is very efficient at keeping the level of sugar in the blood constant, so an athlete taking sugar will not reap any rewards in terms of being able to train longer or recover from training more quickly.

At the end of training schedules athletes often go through mood changes and are frequently at their most irritable or prone to worrying. Being hungry and burning up stores of energy leaves people feeling cross. Such feelings often disappear when the hunger is banished by a drastic measure such as a post-training bar of chocolate. The improved feeling is a temporary one and will reappear as the hunger returns, that is as soon as the liver has removed all the sugar from the blood. All this puts the emphasis on the need to eat a proper balanced meal or even a snack after training.

The 'chocolate bar recovery' syndrome helps no one. It has a long-term damaging effect on recovery.

The athlete's need to supply himself with carbohydrates is critical. But it is the unrefined carbohydrates which come from a wholefood diet which are so important, because they will provide the starch.

The refined carbohydrates – sugar and sugar products, white flour and white flour products – do not help at all. They are empty calories which have lost natural sources of many essential vitamins and minerals.

So it is not only a myth that we need sugar for energy, but a dangerous one. The sad thing is that our taste for sweet things is indulged and nurtured from the time we are children. It seems that we are destined to be addicted from tender years.

Nature intended us to eat sugar with fibre, which means that by eating it in fruits we would in fact eat very little of it. What we have succeeded in doing is to concentrate our need for sugar as part of bulking foods, down to much more powerful doses such as sugar in tea or coffee or sugar put into processed foods.

Sugar is a natural substance which we have refined unnaturally, so that it becomes potentially harmful when taken in large amounts.

In Britain we now eat over 120lbs of sugar per person a year – a frightening amount, especially when you consider that it is of little practical value.

It is hard to cut down on sugar when food manufacturers add it to such a wide range of their products. For example, there is 'hidden' sugar in the following:

Baked beans
Biscuits
Cakes
Canned fruit in syrup
Canned vegetables
Commercial salad dressing
Flavoured fruit yoghurt
Fruit squash
Ice cream
Jams and preserves
Ketchup
Packaged desserts
Pastries
Pickles

Artificial sweeteners in food and drinks are used widely both by the general public and in the food industry. Most artificial sweeteners have no nutritional value and so do not encourage tooth decay or add to the calorie intake – all they do is make the food taste sweet. Recent developments using natural sweeteners have taken off some of the pressures about the safety of saccharine. It all dodges the real issue, though. Cutting down on sweet foods is the only solution.

How to cut down on sugar

- Give up adding sugar to tea or coffee.
- Read food labels. Many manufactured foods have sugar added during processing, for example baked beans and tinned fruit. Avoid products where sugar, liquid glucose, or maize or corn syrup comes near to the top of the list of ingredients. Food labelling regulations demand that ingredients are given in descending order of weight.
- Do not eat chocolate bars or cakes to fill in, or at the end of a training session or game. Fruit is a much better alternative, or even better a sandwich.
- Give up sweet drinks such as squashes and opt for mineral water, or fruit or vegetable juices.
- Do not add sugar to breakfast cereals – add some fresh fruit or natural yoghurt instead.
- Cut down on cakes and biscuits in general. Eat more wholemeal bread.
- Cut back – or even better cut out – jams, marmalades and honeys, which are high in sugar.
- Use spices to add flavourings to desserts rather than sugar.
- Cut out on the sugar-laden desserts and try such things as natural yoghurt, fresh or stewed fruit, or fresh fruit salad without any added sugar.
- Cut down the sugar intake from alcohol and stick to dry wine and dry cider.

Why you have to cut down on salt

More people than ever now know about the importance of fibre and are doing something about it.

With regard to the dangers of too many fats and too much sugar, most of us would probably have some idea if our diets contained too much of either.

However, few would realise the potential for harm which can come from eating too much salt. For, just as we eat too much sugar, so we are also guilty of eating too much salt. We add it to our meals, often before we have even tasted a dish, and too much of it is used in the processing of a wide range of foods.

An excess of salt causes high blood pressure and fluid retention and can lead to much higher risks of heart disease and kidney failure.

Athletes worry about whether they need extra salt in hot weather. Those who do sweat, do lose some sodium, but do not become depleted. Sweat has proportionally less sodium when compared with your blood and intracellular fluid. Replacing the sodium is not as important as replacing the water.

Athletes who train in the heat sweat less sodium but more water than an inactive person. The long-distance runner who trains for 20 miles on a hot summer day may lose anything between 1.85 and 5.50gms of sodium. The amount of sodium actually increases with heavier sweating.

The pressure on your body is to replace the water it has lost, not the salt. So it is important to emphasise the waste and dangers to athletes if they take salt tablets. These are unnecessary and dangerous; they dehydrate your body by drawing water from the body tissues into your stomach in order to dilute the high sodium concentration from the tablet. Restoring the sodium losses which do occur is easy.

The danger to your diet is that you are overdoing the salt. Salt is a combination of two minerals – sodium and chloride. Although some sodium is important for maintaining proper fluid balance between the water in and around the cells and in your blood, too much sodium can lay the foundations for high blood pressure.

In Britain we eat four times the amount of salt we need. The NACNE report, outlining the guidelines for the future British diet, suggests reducing the average salt intake to 3g a day. The current level is put around the 12g a day mark. That may have a connection with another statistic – that almost one in five adults in this country suffer from high blood pressure.

Hence it is vital that athletes should act now and decisively to reduce the amount of salt they eat. Blood pressure is of considerable importance to anyone who is exercising regularly. The levels of blood pressure in the body are constantly changing; they react to stress and to exercise, reaching peaks during periods of activity and then recovering and returning to normal. The measurement of an athlete's blood pressure is an important indicator of performance and one of the first statistics researchers wish to have available.

Team coaches and doctors need to have constant reminders of blood pressure levels in order to monitor a range of performances – and more important, recovery from training.

Any factor which is likely to have such a dramatic effect on blood pressure needs to be monitored carefully, and the effect of salt can be critical. Certainly, cutting back on salt will help people with high blood pressure, as has been proved in extensive tests. The problem in cutting back in the amount you eat falls neatly into two sections, however.

First, you should cut out what you add to your meal at the table. Throw out the salt-shaker. Most of us add the salt through habit rather than from need or because of taste. So get accustomed to tasting the food first. If you are conscious of the need to cut back, then you will find you can do something about it quite easily.

There are salt substitutes and salt replacements on the market. The former eliminates sodium chloride altogether and supplies potassium salts in its place. The low sodium products, including mineral and herb-based salts are a half-way step, aimed at cutting back the amount of sodium while still supplying some of the flavour of the salt.

By becoming more aware of the dangers of salt, you will find it easier than you think to stop taking it. In baking, it is much easier than you might expect to find alternatives which add flavour and texture to your food – sesame and sunflower seeds, oatmeal, herbs – all these can be used to replace the salt.

What it may not be so easy to do is to spot the hidden salt in prepared food. A vast range of convenience foods have salt already added to them and salt and sodium-based additives are also put in many foods. The worst culprits are highly processed foods, where manufacturers are seeking a long shelf-life and they want to add flavour to their products. It is not only a cheap way to win the public's favour with a product, but also the biggest single factor in the high levels of salt in our diet.

So how can you set about checking how much salt you have in your diet?

The rule you have to apply is to make sure you read the list of ingredients on foods. In addition to sodium-based additives, the danger ingredients include monosodium glutamate (MSG), baking powder, brine and sodium bicarbonate.

The labelling requirements for foods in this country demand

that food manufacturers state the additives with specific E numbers. If you are looking for salt-based additives, the following list indicates those which should be avoided wherever possible in your diet.

E201	sodium sorbate
E211	sodium benzoate
E221	sodium sulphite
E222	sodium hydrogen sulphite
E223	sodium metabisulphite
E237	sodium formate
E250	sodium nitrite
E251	sodium nitrate
E262	sodium hydrogen diacetate
E281	sodium propionate
E301	sodium-L-ascorbate
E325	sodium lactate
E331	sodium dihydrogen citrate
E331	diSodium citrate
E331	triSodium citrate
E335	sodium tartrate
E339(a)	sodium dihydrogen orthophosphate
E339(b)	diSodium hydrogen orthophosphate
E339(c)	triSodium orthophosphate
E401	sodium alginate
E450(a)	diSodium dihydrogen diphosphate
E450(a)	tetraSodium diphosphate
E450(b)	pentaSodium triphosphate
E450(c)	sodium polyphosphates
E466	carboxymethylcellulose, sodium salt
E470	sodium, potassium and calcium salts of fatty acids
E481	sodium stearoyl-2-lactylate

A quick guide as to the kinds of foods which contain a lot of salt is fairly easy to give.

High sodium foods include bacon, ham, beefburgers, almost all processed and preserved meats, smoked fish, smoked salmon, smoked haddock, all hard cheeses, salted butter and margarines, self-raising flour, tomato sauce, baking powder, most sweet biscuits, salted nuts, crisps and other snack products. The list is wide, but the important thing is that by taking some action on cutting back on these foods, you will achieve a significant effect on the amount of salt which is going into your diet.

Low sodium foods which it is desirable to aim for include tea and decaffeinated coffee, nuts, wholemeal flour and pasta, brown rice, unsalted butter and low salt margarines, fresh fruit, vegetables (apart from spinach, celery, carrots, radishes and beetroot which have some natural sodium in them), red and rosé wines.

Recipes for you to eat to win

SAVOURIES

CASHEW NUT PATTIES
90gCHO, 1300 cals. in total

1 medium onion, chopped
yeast extract
1½oz (40g) wholemeal flour
⅓ pint (185ml) liquid skimmed milk
5oz (150g) cashew nuts, ground
1oz (25g) cashew nuts, chopped
2 teaspoonsful lemon juice
seasoning
natural bran to coat

Serves 4
Cook onions until tender by stirring in a little yeast extract. Add a little of the cold milk to the flour to form a paste and heat the remainder of the milk. Put in the hot milk to the blended flour, mix well and add to the onions. Stir the milk over the heat for a few minutes to thicken and then add the cashew nuts, lemon juice and seasoning. Continue to cook for three minutes, then leave the mixture to cool on a wet plate.
Divide into 8 and coat with bran to form patties.
Fry in a non-stick pan or grill to crisp both sides and heat through.

TWO BEAN SAVOURY
150gCHO, 1300 cals. in total

4oz (100g) red kidney beans
4oz (100g) butter beans
1 large onion, finely chopped

94

yeast extract
1oz (25g) wholemeal flour
1 large tin tomatoes
$\frac{1}{2}$ teaspoonful dried oregano
2 tablespoonsful tomato purée
4oz (100g) grated cheese
1oz (25g) walnuts, chopped
fresh parsley, chopped, to garnish

Serves 4
Drain both portions of beans.
Sauté the onion in a little yeast extract until tender.
Drain the tomatoes and use a little of the juice to mix with the flour to form a paste.
Heat the rest of the tomato juice, slowly add it to the blended flour and return to the heat.
Add the onions, beans, drained tomatoes, herbs, purée and seasoning.
Simmer the bean mixture, covered, for about 10 minutes and then spoon into a warmed dish.
Arrange the cheese in a line down the dish, sprinkling the nuts on top.
Place under a hot grill to melt the cheese and to brown the topping.
Garnish with the parsley.

'NO TIME' PIZZA
90gCHO, 780 cals. in total

4oz (100g) self-raising wholemeal flour
$\frac{1}{2}$ teaspoonful sea salt
1 large onion, chopped finely
1 teaspoonful dried oregano/basil
$\frac{1}{2}$lb (225g) tomatoes, skinned and chopped
seasoning
4oz (100g) medium fat cheese, grated

Serves 2
Mix the flour and the salt together and then add sufficient water (about 3–4 tablespoonsful) to form a stiff dough.
Press out into a 7-in. (18cm) round and fry in a non-stick frying pan for about 5–6 minutes.

Meanwhile prepare the topping by cooking the onions, herbs, tomatoes and seasonings together until the onions are tender and some of the liquid has evaporated.

Turn the dough over in the pan and spread the topping, alternately with the cheese, on to the base.

Cook in the pan for another 5–6 minutes, popping the pizza under a hot grill to get a bubbling topping before serving.

PEANUT AND VEGETABLE CURRY
70gCHO, 1400 cals. in total

6oz (175g) peanuts
4 medium onions, chopped
1 dessertspoonful curry powder
1 teaspoonful garam masala
1 teaspoonful ginger, ground
2 cloves garlic
1 tablespoonful wholemeal flour
1lb (450g) vegetables, chopped, e.g. cauliflower, mushrooms, peppers
⅔ pint (370ml) liquid skimmed milk
seasoning

Serves 4

Soak and cook the peanuts (1 hour soaking and then 30 minutes in a pressure cooker, or overnight soaking and 2–3 hours cooking).

Gently cook the onions, curry powder, garam masala, ginger and garlic in a non-stick pan until the onions are tender.

Make a paste with the flour and a little of the milk.

Heat the rest of the milk and slowly add to the paste, mixing well. Pour the milk and flour mix over the onions, add peanuts and seasoning and cook for about 15–20 minutes, stirring occasionally and adding the vegetables towards the end.

Serve garnished with slices of raw tomato or cucumber.

ENGLISH BRAN MUFFINS
240gCHO, 1340 cals. in total

10oz (275g) wholemeal flour
1 teaspoonful baking powder

4oz (100g) bran
2oz (50g) fructose
½ teaspoonful ground cinnamon
pinch ground cloves
pinch nutmeg
½pt skimmed milk
2 egg whites

Makes 15 muffins
Sift flour and baking powder and add in the bran.
Mix together all the dry ingredients.
Combine the milk and add to the dry ingredients.
Beat the egg whites until stiff, but not dry, and fold into the bran mixture.
Spoon into a greased bun tin and bake at 400°F/200°C (Gas mark 6) for 20 minutes.

SUMMER VEGETABLE STEW
180gCHO 1350 cals. in total

1 tablespoon oil
1 large onion, chopped
1 clove garlic, crushed
1 medium aubergine, cubed
6 tomatoes, cut up, or tin tomatoes
1–2 tablespoons sugar or molasses
½ teaspoon basil
pepper
salt
½ cup cheddar or swiss cheese, grated

Serves 4
Sauté the onion in oil, in a large pan.
Add the remaining ingredients except cheese. Cover, cook for 20 minutes or until tender.
Put into shallow baking dish. Sprinkle with cheese.
Optional: brown under the grill before serving.

ADZUKI BEAN SALAD
160gCHO 810 cals. in total

2 cupsful rice, cooked
4oz (100g) adzuki beans
1 large green pepper, chopped and de-seeded
2 stalks of celery, finely chopped
½ cucumber, diced
6 spring onions, chopped

Serves 2
Soak beans overnight and cook until tender (about an hour).
Mix the dressing in a salad bowl. Add the cooked rice and beans
straight into the dressing. Turn lightly with a fork and leave to
cool. Mix in the chopped vegetables. Taste and season with salt
and pepper.

BRAZIL NUT AND RICE RISSOLES
180gCHO 350 cals. per serving

12oz (300g) cooked rice
6oz (175g) milled or finely chopped Brazil nuts
1 tablespoon butter
1 medium onion, finely diced
1 teaspoon sage
salt and black pepper to taste
1 egg, beaten
oil for frying

Serves 4
Combine the rice and chopped nuts. Sauté the onion in the butter
until soft and golden.
Mix together the rice and nut mixture, onion, sage and salt and
black pepper to taste.
Add the beaten egg and form the mixture into oblong rissoles.
Fry them golden brown in hot oil and serve with a cheese or
tomato sauce or as an accompaniment to cooked vegetables.

WALNUT AND POTATO PATTIES
190gCHO 1470 cals. in total

12oz (300g) mashed potato
6oz (175g) finely chopped walnuts

4oz (100g) fine breadcrumbs
1 teaspoon mixed herbs
grated rind of ½ lemon
2 tablespoons finely chopped onion
salt and black pepper to taste
8fl oz (1 cup) milk, chilled
oil for frying

Serves 4–6
Combine the first 7 ingredients and add enough milk to form a malleable mixture. Form into circular patties.
Fry golden brown in hot oil or deep fry.
Serve with sauce and a green salad garnished with tomatoes.

RICE WITH SPINACH
125gCHO 380 cals. per serving

½lb (225g) spinach, washed, chopped
4 tablespoons butter
1 medium onion diced
4fl oz (120ml) natural yoghurt
1 teaspoon cinnamon
salt and black pepper to taste
1lb (450g) parboiled, long-grain rice
1 egg, beaten

Serves 6–8
Preheat oven to 350°F (Gas mark 4). Boil the spinach in a little water (1 or 2 tablespoons) for 6–8 minutes. Drain and squeeze out excess water.
Heat the butter in a heavy frying pan and sauté the onion for 2 minutes. Add the spinach and sauté, stirring, for a further 2–4 minutes.
Pour the mixture into a bowl and stir in the yoghurt and cinnamon.
Season to taste with salt and black pepper.
Combine ⅓ of the rice with the beaten egg and cover the bottom of a 9-inch casserole with the mixture.
Now make alternate layers of the spinach/yoghurt mixture and the remaining rice, ending up with a layer of rice.
Cover and bake for 30 minutes.
   Alternatively this dish can be steamed. Prepare the layers of rice

and spinach mixture in a heavy pan. Cover with a tight-fitting lid and cook for 45–60 minutes over a very low heat. This is the more genuine way to cook the dish.

ADZUKI AND CAULIFLOWER FLAN
90gCHO 1740 cals. in total

8oz (225g) Weetabix or similar
4oz (100g) polyunsaturated margarine
1 small cauliflower
4oz (100g) cooked adzuki beans
1oz (25g) wholemeal flour
1oz (25g) polyunsaturated margarine
¼ pint (140ml) milk
seasoning to taste

Serves 4
Take the flakes, melt the 4oz (100g) margarine and combine it with the crumbs. Press into a small flan dish, taking it up the sides as well as on the base. Set aside to cool.
Cook the cauliflower florets briefly in boiling water, drain. Mix with the drained beans.
Make a fairly thick sauce by heating 1oz (25g) margarine, adding the flour and then the milk and cooking for a few minutes; season.
Turn the cauliflower and beans into the sauce, mix well, then place in the prepared flan case.
Heat through for 15 minutes at 350°F/180°C (Gas Mark 4).

LEEK PAELLA
90gCHO 1540 cals. in total

8oz (225g) leeks
4 medium tomatoes
6oz (75g) brown rice
2oz (50g) polyunsaturated margarine
1 pint (½ litre) vegetable stock or water
seasoning to taste
2 tablespoonsful tahini or 2oz (50g) toasted flaked almonds
seasoning to taste

Serves 4

Remove the outer and wilted leaves of the leeks, cut off the base.
Cut into sections about 1in. long.

Melt the margarine, add the leeks and cook gently for 3 minutes,
stirring occasionally.

Add the rice and fry for a few minutes longer.

Stir in the liquid, quartered tomatoes and seasoning. Bring to the
boil, cover and simmer until the rice is cooked (approximately 30
minutes).

If using tahini, stir it in before serving the rice. Nuts can be
sprinkled on top of individual portions.

POTATO AND WALNUT LOAF
140gCHO 990 cals. in total
Time: 40 minutes

4 large cooked potatoes (left-overs are ideal)
1 large green pepper
4oz (100g) walnut pieces
2 eggs
2 teaspoonsful mixed herbs
2 tablespoonsful wholemeal breadcrumbs
½oz (15g) polyunsaturated margarine
seasoning to taste

Serves 4

Mash the potatoes; chop the pepper finely; beat the eggs.

Combine all these with the nuts, herbs and seasoning, and transfer
to a lightly greased loaf tin.

Top with the breadcrumbs and dot with margarine.

Bake at 350°F/180°C (Gas Mark 4) for 30 minutes.

CAULIFLOWER AND POTATO SAVOURY
130gCHO 1050 cals. in total

4 medium potatoes, cooked
1 medium cauliflower
2 large tomatoes
½ pint (140ml) water in which 1 teaspoonful yeast extract has
been dissolved

101

1oz (25g) polyunsaturated margarine
seasoning to taste
Parmesan cheese

Serves 4
Break the cauliflower into florets and fry them gently in the melted margarine for a few minutes.
Add the water and yeast extract, plus the sliced potatoes and quartered tomatoes. Stir them gently together.
Bring the liquid to the boil, then cover the pan and simmer for 5 minutes.
Serve with Parmesan cheese.

CHEESY EGGS
90gCHO 280 cals. in total

2 eggs
1oz (25g) hard cheese – Cheddar or Double Gloucester
1oz (25g) fine wholemeal breadcrumbs
knob of margarine
sea salt and freshly ground black pepper
a few sesame seeds

Serves 2
Break eggs into a bowl and stir slowly with a fork so that the eggs are just mixed, not beaten.
Cut the butter into tiny pieces and add to the egg. Grate the cheese, and mix in well. Add the salt, pepper and breadcrumbs and mix in thoroughly.
Turn the mixture into a well greased ovenproof dish.
Sprinkle sesame seeds on the top and bake in a moderate oven. Individual dishes should take about 10–15 minutes, whereas a larger dish will take a little longer.

MIXED BEAN SALAD
160gCHO 820 cals. in total

4oz (100g) dried kidney beans
4oz (100g) chick peas
4oz (100g) haricot beans
4oz (100g) brown rice, cooked

1lb (450g) sliced green beans
2 onions

Serves 2
Soak pulses overnight, then cook for 1½–2 hours – separately if convenient.
Cook green beans in salted water till tender but not too soft. Slice onions into rings.
Drain beans and green beans as well. Mix in a bowl with onions and pour on vinaigrette. Cool.

CHEESE AND BARLEY PUDDING
140gCHO 1200 cals. in total

1pt (575ml) milk
4oz (100g) whole barley
1oz (25g) butter
2 eggs, separated
4oz (100g) grated cheese
½ teaspoon salt
¼ teaspoon black pepper
pinch cinnamon
pinch nutmeg

Serves 4
Preheat oven to 375°F (Gas mark 5). Bring the milk to boiling.
Pour it over the barley and set aside for 30 minutes.
Now add the butter to the barley and milk and beat in the egg yolks and cheese.
Season and then fold in the well-beaten egg whites.
Transfer the mixture to a greased baking dish and bake for 30–40 minutes or until the barley is cooked.

LENTIL AND BARLEY RISSOLES
180gCHO 360 cals. per person

1lb (450g) cooked, drained whole barley
8oz (225g) cooked, drained, split red lentils
4oz (100g) cheese, grated
1 egg, beaten
1 tablespoon tomato purée

1 teaspoon salt
½ teaspoon black pepper
½ teaspoon dried thyme
about 2oz (50g) wholemeal flour
oil for frying

Serves 4
Combine all the ingredients, adding enough flour to form a
mixture of such consistency that it will hold its shape.
Form the mixture into 3-inch-long oval rissoles.
Fry them golden brown in hot oil.

BARLEY SQUARES
160gCHO 1150 cals. in total

1 tablespoon vegetable oil
1 medium onion, diced
1 stick celery, diced
2 tablespoons parsley, chopped
4oz (100g) whole barley, soaked overnight, drained
4 fl oz milk
1 teaspoon salt
½ teaspoon black pepper
2oz (50g) cheese, grated
1 egg, beaten
1 tablespoon milk
oil for frying

Serves 4
Heat the oil in a heavy frying pan. Add the onion, celery, parsley
and barley and stir-fry until all the vegetables are soft.
Add the milk and cook until all the liquid is absorbed by the
barley.
Add the salt, black pepper and cheese and mix well.Turn the
mixture onto a wetted board and press it into a square about ½-
inch thick. Leave to cool.
Cut into 2-inch squares. Beat the egg and one tablespoon of milk
together.
Dip squares in egg and milk and fry in hot oil, browning both
sides.

SWEETS

BANANA SURPRISE
80gCHO 310 cals.

1 egg
1 heaped teaspoonful honey
1 banana
1 slice lemon
a little oil for cooking

Serves 1
Beat the egg well, mix in the honey.
Grate the banana on a cheese grater and add it to the egg mixture.
Put the oil into a saucepan and put on a medium heat. When the oil is sizzling pour the banana mix into the saucepan and start stirring immediately with a wooden spoon.
Cook for one or two minutes, stirring all the time, until the egg appears cooked and the scent of the banana cooking starts wafting about. Put the mixture into a warmed serving bowl and put the lemon slice on the top. Serve straight away.

GRILLED GRAPEFRUIT
50gCHO

1 grapefruit
2 teaspoonsful clear honey
2 knobs of margarine
2 slices wholewheat bread spread lightly with margarine

Serves 2
Cut the grapefruit in half and remove the obvious pips.
Trickle the honey over each cut surface as evenly as you can.
Put some margarine on each half in the centre and put the grapefruit under a hot grill for a few minutes to cook.
Serve hot with triangles of wholewheat bread.

GRAPE CRUNCH
120gCHO 210 cals. per person

6oz (175g) grapes
1oz (25g) cashew nuts

4oz (100g) wheat flakes
3oz (75g) breadcrumbs
1 generous tablespoonful honey
1oz (25g) margarine
1 level tablespoonful 85 per cent wheatmeal flour

Serves 3–4

Melt the butter in a saucepan, add the cashew nuts and the wheat flakes and cook them gently in the butter until it has all been soaked up.

Add the honey, stir well, and cook for a further minute or two. Take the pips out of the grapes and put them in a saucepan with 1 tablespoonful boiling water.

Simmer gently for a couple of minutes until they go soft, but not mushy. Add the flour and stir well, still on a medium heat, until thickened.

Combine with mixture, adding breadcrumbs and mixing everything together thoroughly.

Leave this overnight at room temperature. In the morning it will all be stuck together, so break it up with a fork into bite-sized pieces. Divide the mixture out between three or four bowls, pour milk over each one and serve.

FRUITY CHEESECAKE
90gCHO 1170 cals. in total

2 large oranges
6 wholemeal biscuits
grated rind 1 lemon
12oz (300g) curd cheese
2 eggs, beaten
1 tablespoonful concentrated natural unsweetened orange juice

Serves 4–6

Grate the rind of the oranges.

Crumble the biscuits and sprinkle over the base of a non-stick flan tin, ideally loose-bottomed.

Blend together the orange and lemon rind, cheese, eggs and fruit juice and pour the mixture carefully onto the crumb base.

Bake for 45 minutes at 350°F/180°C (Gas Mark 4), then cool and remove from tin.

Decorate with slices of fresh orange.

Exactly the same weight of fruit such as peaches, apples and pears can be used.

BAKED BANANAS
70gCHO 380 cals. in total

6 small bananas
juice 2 oranges
1 tablespoonful rum
1 tablespoonful desiccated coconut, toasted

Serves 4–6
Split the bananas in half and place in a shallow dish.
Mix the orange juice and rum and pour over.
Bake at 300°F/150°C (Gas Mark 2) for about 20 minutes, basting occasionally.
Serve sprinkled with the toasted coconut.

High protein diets

This diet provides about twice the amount of protein normally required daily. It is crucial when extra physical activity is undertaken.

The protein sources are 2pt (1.13 litres) milk daily, 8oz (225g) high-quality animal protein (meat or poultry), provided that 12oz (340g) fish can substitute for 8oz (225g) lean meat. Cheese is reckoned as approximately equivalent to meat, while 1 whole egg can substitute for 1oz (25g) meat. Further protein sources are bread, cereals and beans.

At least 8 slices of bread and 2 cupsful of cereal are included. Fruit and vegetables are unrestricted.

There are diets for one and seven days.

High protein diet for one day

Breakfast   Tea or coffee with milk
Cereal with milk
2 eggs cooked as preferred or 2oz (57g) bacon, ham
    or 3oz (85g) fish
2oz (57g) bread, toasted if required
Butter or margarine
Jam, honey, marmalade, syrup or Marmite

Elevenses   Milk with or without cereals

Lunch   Vegetable soup
3oz (85g) meat, liver, ham, poultry or 4½oz (127g)
    fish or cheese
Potato and green or root vegetables or salad
Fruit, pudding or custard made up from milk and
    eggs with flour
Tea or coffee with milk

Tea	Tea or coffee with milk
	2oz (50g) brown or white bread
	Butter or margarine
	2oz (50g) cheese or meat or 2 eggs
	Salad

Dinner	Soup, vegetable or lentils or beans
	3oz (75g) meat or cheese or 4½oz (127g) fish or 3 eggs
	Vegetables and/or potatoes
	2oz (50g) brown or white bread
	Butter or margarine
	Fruit with cheese
	Tea or coffee with milk

Bedtime	Milk drink

A six-day plan for high protein–low cholesterol diet

Day 1

Breakfast	Grilled mushrooms and tomatoes
	2 halves toast with low fat margarine
	Brewer's yeast or wheatgerm

Lunch	Orange or pineapple slice
	Salad with 2 slices lean chicken
	2 crispbreads and low fat margarine

Dinner	Grapefruit
	Steamed cod or haddock
	French or runner beans
	Sprouts or cauliflower
	2oz (50g) cottage cheese mixed with grapes

Day 2

Breakfast	2 oranges or 2 apples
	2 thin slices wholemeal toast with low fat margarine and a little honey

Lunch	Orange or pineapple slice
	Salad with 3oz (75g) cottage cheese
	2 crispbreads and low fat margarine

Dinner	Grapefruit
	Steamed hake or sole

Broccoli or cauliflower
2 crispbreads with cottage cheese spread

Day 3
Breakfast Apple

Lunch Orange or pineapple

Dinner Grapefruit **or**

Breakfast Grilled tomatoes on toast, 2 crispbreads or extra slice toast and low fat margarine. Dried apricots with wheatgerm

Lunch Salad with flaked fish in oil and onion and tomato slices. 2 crispbreads with low fat margarine

Dinner Casserole of veal or chicken with diced vegetables. Baked apple with cottage cheese centre

Day 4
Breakfast Apple
Mushrooms on toast with extra slice toast and low fat margarine
Few soaked raisins with wheatgerm

Lunch Orange or pineapple
Salad
3oz (75g) cottage cheese with 2 crispbreads

Dinner Grapefruit
Steamed haddock or cod
Root vegetable
Spinach or French beans
2oz (50g) plain yoghurt

Day 5
Breakfast Apple
Pineapple (dried) with wheatgerm
2 slices wholemeal toast and low fat margarine

Lunch Orange
Salad with hard-boiled egg
2 crispbreads and low fat margarine

Dinner Grapefruit
Turkey or chicken or lean beef

Grilled Tomatoes
Onions or leeks
2oz (50g) plain yoghurt

Day 6

Breakfast   Apple (grated) with wheatgerm
Orange
2 crispbreads with low fat margarine

Lunch   Orange or pineapple
Salad with flaked fish in oil and onion and tomato
slices
2 crispbreads with low fat margarine

Dinner   Grapefruit
Lean lamb or chicken slices
Aubergine or marrow
French beans or spinach
2oz (50g) plain yoghurt

Salad recipes

In the high protein diet proper, some proteins in the salads have too high a cholesterol content for the person who requires a high protein-low cholesterol diet. The following salads can be safely used by those who need to watch cholesterol content, though they can also be adopted generally. They are based on servings for two.

High protein – low cholesterol

Raw Cabbage Salad

Shred ¼ small raw cabbage (red or green) and add 1 tablespoon cider vinegar. Allow to stand for 3–4 hours. Add a small sliced raw onion or leek, one coarsely grated raw apple and herbs to taste.

Carrot and Cheese and Celery Salad

Grate one large raw carrot, add 4 sticks sliced celery, 2oz (50g) cottage cheese, 1 orange (sliced), ½ green or red pepper and 1 tablespoon of cider vinegar and oil dressing.

Pineapple Salad

Two slices pineapple or cubes, ½ green or red pepper, one small grated raw beetroot, 1oz (25g) cottage cheese, 6 sprigs of raw cauliflower. Mix and serve with cider vinegar and oil dressing with mint added.

Tomato and French Bean Salad

Slice 2 large tomatoes and add one cup cooked French or runner beans, ½ sliced onion, ¼ sliced cucumber and ¼ green or red pepper. Mix with cider vinegar and oil dressing.

Green Salad

A quarter shredded lettuce or endive, one bunch watercress, 4 spring onions or half a sliced leek and six radishes with green tops. Dandelion or nasturtium leaves. Decorate with slices of lemon or orange.

Beetroot Salad

Coarsely grate one medium beetroot and mix with 1 tablespoon cider vinegar and little oil. Add chives or sliced onion and parsley. Lay mixture on a bed of lettuce or watercress and decorate with slices of pineapple or peach. Add cottage cheese topping.

Cucumber Salad

One-third unpeeled cucumber sliced and mixed with 1 tablespoon yoghurt. Lemon juice to taste. Add ½ a sliced red or green pepper, chives or a smear of garlic and chopped parsley. Serve on a layer of lettuce, endive or watercress and decorate with slices of tomato, and sprigs of cauliflower or asparagus.

Root Salad

One medium raw carrot, 1 small or ½ medium raw beetroot, 1 small celeriac or celery root. Coarsely grate the roots and mix with cider vinegar and oil. Add parsley, thyme and mint. Mix and serve on a bed of sliced tomato and decorate with the strips of pineapple.

Winter Salad

A quarter shredded cabbage, $\frac{1}{2}$ small onion, 4 sticks celery, 1 medium raw carrot. Grate the carrot, shred the other vegetables and mix with cider vinegar and oil. Mix and decorate with slices of orange and small knobs of cottage cheese.

Quick Salad

One medium carrot cut in thin strips with 2 sliced tomatoes, sprigs of cauliflower, $\frac{1}{2}$ green or red pepper and 1oz (25g) cottage cheese.

APPENDIX 1:
Guidelines for a new eating to win plan

- Eat brown or preferably wholemeal bread rather than white. When you make sandwiches, try to have more bread and less filling in each one.

- Substitute wholewheat flour (or near relation) for white in home-made bread, pastries, cakes, biscuits.

- Look for wholemeal pasta, such as spaghetti and macaroni, also wholewheat or bran crispbreads; and brown unpolished rice (this takes longer to cook than white rice – approximately $\frac{3}{4}$ hour).

- Digestive biscuits are made from wholewheat flour.

- Choose fibre-rich breakfast cereals, many of which are described using the word 'bran'.

- Boil or bake potatoes in their skins.

- Eat nuts and dried fruits. Use lentils, beans and peas.

- Eat meat no more than once a day and, when you do, eat it sparingly. About 4oz (120g) is quite sufficient for an adult.

- Cut out fatty parts of meat. Leanest meats are chicken and turkey.

- White fish is less fatty than others such as mackerel, salmon or sardines, and has fewer calories than meat for weight.

- Use butter sparingly. Add less cream to puddings and reduce sugar as much as possible.

- Grill instead of fry: use non-stick pans for frying with minimum fat.

114

- Brown sugar has little more nutritional value than white; both are termed 'empty calories' because they provide energy but virtually nothing else.

- When possible, eat fresh rather than canned fruit. The latter usually has a high sugar content.

- Drink sweetened drinks sparingly. They have a high sugar content.

- Reduce salt in diet by using sparingly in cooking, seldom adding more when eating. Smoked fish and meats have a high salt content.

APPENDIX 2:
How many calories you can burn off in different activities

Activity	Calories Per Hour
A. Rest and Light Activity	50–200
Lying down or sleeping	80
Sitting	100
Driving a car	120
Standing	140
Domestic Work	180
B. Moderate Activity	200–350
Bicycling (5½mph)	210
Walking (2½mph)	210
Gardening	220
Canoeing (2½mph)	230
Golf	250
Lawn mowing (power mower)	250
Lawn mowing (hand mower)	270
Bowling	270
Fencing	300
Rowing (2½mph)	300
Swimming (¼mph)	300
Walking (3¼mph)	300
Badminton	350
Horseback riding (trotting)	350
Square-dancing	350
Volleyball	350
Roller skating	350
C. Vigorous Activity	over 350
Table tennis	360
Ditch digging (hand shovel)	400
Ice skating (10mph)	400

Wood chopping or sawing	400
Tennis	420
Water skiing	480
Hill climbing (100ft per hr)	490
Skiing (10mph)	600
Squash and handball	600
Bicycling (13mph)	660
Scull rowing (race)	840
Running (10mph)	900

APPENDIX 3:
The vitamins you need – and where to get them

Vitamin	Best food sources	Function	Deficiency signs	Minimum daily need
A retinol	Fish liver oil, oily fish, liver, kidney, dairy foods, margarine, green vegetables, yellow fruit	Essential for growth, health of eyes, structure and health of skin	Low resistance to infection, night blindness, catarrhal and bronchial infections, skin complaints	Children under 13 : 1200iu (=360mcg) Adults: 2,500iu (=750mcg)
B1 thiamine	Yeast, wheat germ, meat, soya beans, whole grain foods, green vegetables	Essential for growth, conversion of carbohydrates into energy, health of nerves, muscles	Nervous disorders, skin and hair disorders, depression, poor digestion	Children under 13 : 0.8mg Adults: 1–1.2mg
B2 riboflavin	Yeast, wheat germ, meat, soya beans, eggs, vegetables	Essential for growth, health of skin, mouth, eyes, general well-being	Dry hair and skin, mouth sores, nervousness, lack of stamina	Children under 13 : 0.8mg Adults: 1.7mg
B5 pantothenic acid	Yeast, liver, wholemeal bread, brown rice, eggs	Health of skin and hair, including hair growth. Needed for all tissue growth	Dry skin and hair	Children under 13 : 2.5mg Adults: 5–10mg
B6 pyridoxine	Yeast, wheat germ, meat, fish, wholemeal products, milk, cabbage	Essential for body's use of protein, health of skin, nerves and muscle	Irritability, depression, skin eruptions, insomnia, muscle cramps	2mg. Women taking oral contraceptives need much more
B12 cobalamins or cyanocobalamin	Liver and meat, spinach, eggs, lettuce	Health of nerves and skin, body's use of protein, growth	Anaemia, tiredness, skin disorders	Children under 13: 0.5–1mcg Adults: 1–5mcg

Vitamin	Best food sources	Function	Deficiency signs	Minimum daily need
biotin (B group)	Liver, kidney, vegetables, nuts	Probably essential for healthy skin, nerves and muscle	Falling hair, eczema	Children under 13: 0.25mcg Adults: 1mcg
choline and inositol (B group)	Eggs, liver, yeast, offal	Both essential for functioning of liver, prevent build-up of fats in body	Liver disorders, reduced alcohol tolerance	Children under 13: 2.5mg Adults: 10mg of each
folic acid (B group)	Offal meats, green vegetables, yeast	Essential for all growth, healthy blood, fertility	Anaemia, weakness, depression, diarrhoea	0.5mg
niacin nicotinic acid (B group)	Fish, poultry, yeast, peanuts	Essential for growth, health of skin, digestion of carbohydrates, nervous system	Skin disorders, nervous and intestinal upsets, headaches, insomnia	Children under 13: 5–16mg Adults: 18mg
C ascorbic acid	Citrus and other fruit, raw vegetables	Essential to health of cells, blood vessels, gums and teeth, healing of wounds	Sore gums, low resistance to infection, slow healing, painful joints	30mg is minimum
D calciferol	Fish liver oils, sunshine on skin, oily fish, butter and margarine, eggs	Formation of bones and teeth, needed for calcium and phosphorus use	Retarded growth, crooked bones (rickets), tooth decay, weak muscles	Children under 13: 250iu (=10mcg) Adults: 100iu (=2.5mcg)
E tocopherol	Vegetable oils, wheat germ, wholemeal bread, egg yolks, green vegetables, nuts	Known to be essential, but function not fully understood. Needed for fertility and muscle health by animals	In animals, muscular disorders, infertility and nervous disorders	Not certain but estimate at 10iu (=10mg)
K	Green vegetables, soya beans, liver, oils	Essential for blood clotting	Prolonged bleeding from cuts or sores	About 100mcg

APPENDIX 4:
Amino acids

Name	Standard abbreviation
Glycine	Gly
Alanine	Ala
Valine E	Val
Leucine E	Leu
Isoleucine E	Ile
Serine E	Ser
Threonine E	Thr
Aspartic acid	Asp
Glutamic acid	Glu
Lysine E	Lys
Ornithine	Orn
Arginine	Arg
Histidine	His
Phenylalanine E	Phe
Tyrosine	Tyr
Tryptophan E	Trp
Cysteine	Cys
Methionine E	Met
Proline	Pro
Hydroxyproline	Hyp

There is no recommended daily intake for amino acids. The E indicates the essential amino acids which are vital for life. Amino acids are available in a balanced diet but recent research has shown that athletic performance can be improved by the use of supplements. (see Appendix 5)

APPENDIX 5:
Sports supplements suppliers and manufacturers

ALLSPORTS
Health Product Supplies,
43 Balby Road,
Doncaster.

Products: protein powders, energy and protein drinks, weight gain preparations, liquid amino acids, amino acid tablets, liquid and desiccated liver, vitamin, mineral and other nutritional tablets.

DAVINA
Davina Health Products,
1 Cambridge Court,
Cambridge Street,
Sheffield S1 4HN.

Products: weight gain formulas, protein powders, tablets and drinks, liquid amino acids, lecithin powder, energy preparations and drinks, liquid liver, desiccated liver and liver granules, mineral, vitamin and other nutritional supplements.

G. R. LANE'S LECIGRAN
G. R. Lane,
Sissons Road,
Gloucester.

Products: lecithin granules popular with body builders.

MR POWER
Power Health,
10 Central Avenue,
Airfield Estate,
Pocklington,
Yorkshire T4 2DE

Products: protein powders, muscle tonics, vitamin and mineral supplements, lecithin preparations, desiccated liver, amino acid tablets.

SPORTIVE PERFORM
Wander,
Station Road,
King's Langley,
Hertfordshire WD4 8LJ

Products: protein powder, energy drink and bar, multi-mineral preparation, pre-training nutritional food, rapid recovery formula.

SPORTSCRAFT
Booker Health Foods,
45 Station Approach,
West Byfleet,
Surrey.

Products: rapid recovery, electrolyte and energy drinks, muscle build protein.

SURF CITY
English Grains Marketing,
Swains Park,
Park Road,
Overseal,
near Burton-on-Trent.

Products: protein powder, energy drink, desiccated liver, multi-vitamins and minerals and other nutritional supplements.

ULTIMATE NUTRITION
Europa International,
47/49 Talbot Road,
Blackpool,
Lancashire.

Products: weight gain formulas, protein powders and other muscle building preparations, digestive aids, energy and stamina supplements, weight loss and muscle definition products, general health supplements.

WEIDER
Craven House Marketing,
Craven House,
Godalming,
Surrey GU7 1JD.

Products: weight gain formulas, protein powders, liquid amino acids, stamina and energy products, muscle building and muscle definition preparations, vitamin, mineral and other nutritional supplements.